# INTRODUCING PROCESS EXCELLENCE TO YOUR PRACTICE

# DWANE LAY

ISBN-13: 978-1481914208

ISBN-10: 1481914200

You can learn more about the author and his work at www.leanhrblog.com, or you can contact Dwane Lay at dwane.lay@gmail.com.

To my parents, for allowing me to grow up an inquizitive child.

To my wife, for dealing with an adult that can't sit still.

To my sister, because I said I would (even if she doesn't remember it)
and for trying to teach me humility.

And to my boys, for giving me a taste of my own medicine.

"HUNTER S. THOMPSON, BOB GUCCIONE, ANDY WARHOL AND DWANE LAY WERE HAVING LUNCH ONE DAY AT A LOCAL DINER... DWANE WAS REGALING THE GROUP WITH HIS MOST RECENT TRANSATLANTIC EXPLOITS WHEN THE SUBJECT OF THIS BOOK CAME UP. HE TOLD THEM WHAT I'LL TELL YOU. TWO WORDS... LIFE CHANGING. THAT'S ALL FOLKS... BUY IT, READ IT, LIVE IT, SHARE IT. DO YOURSELF AND HUMANITY A FAVOR. BY THE WAY, BOB PICKED UP THE CHECK THAT MORNING. HE'S THAT GUY."

William Tincup, SPHR, CEO | Tincup & Co. | @williamtincup

"WHAT IF YOU COULD GET RID OF THE PROCESSES AND PROCEDURES THAT WASTE YOUR TIME AND MAKE YOUR JOB HARDER? WHAT IF YOU COULD THINK ABOUT THE WAY YOU WORK IN A NEW WAY, A WAY THAT MAKES YOU BETTER AND MORE EFFECTIVE AT WHAT YOU DO? WHAT IF ALL THIS EVEN SAVED TIME, RESOURCES, AND MONEY? AND WHAT IF THERE WERE EVEN ELEPHANT JOKES? DWANE LAY'S EXPERIENCE, SENSIBILITY AND GREAT SENSE OF HUMOR SHOW YOU HOW TO START AND HOW TO GET THERE."

Heather Bussing, Employment Attorney | @heatherbussing

"ONE THING HR ISN'T GREAT AT IS TAKING THE BS OUT OF ANY PROCESS. HR PEOPLE ARE FAMOUS FOR ADDING STRUCTURE AND PROCESS TO JUST ABOUT ANYTHING, WITH THE RATIONALIZATION THAT IT MAKES THE TARGET "MORE FAIR" OR "EASIER TO USE". THAT'S WHERE DWANE LAY COMES IN. A CLASSICALLY TRAINED SIX SIGMA NINJA, DWANE TURNS "LEAN" CONCEPTS INTO EASY TO UNDERSTAND TOOLS TO HELP HR PROS GET TO WHAT'S REAL — AND WHAT PEOPLE WILL ACTUALLY USE. HIGHLY RECOMMENDED!"

Kris Dunn, Chief Human Resources Officer | Kinetix
Founder of blogs: The HR Capitalist and Fistful of Talent | @kris_dunn

# CONTENTS

"WE ARE HERE TO MAKE ANOTHER WORLD."

W. Edwards Deming (1900 - 1993)

"HERE'S TO THE CRAZY ONES. THE MISFITS. THE REBELS. THE
TROUBLEMAKERS. THE ROUND PEGS IN THE SQUARE HOLES.

THE ONES WHO SEE THINGS DIFFERENTLY. THEY'RE NOT FOND OF RULES.
AND THEY HAVE NO RESPECT FOR THE STATUS QUO. YOU CAN QUOTE THEM,
DISAGREE WITH THEM, GLORIFY OR VILIFY THEM.

ABOUT THE ONLY THING YOU CAN'T DO IS IGNORE THEM. BECAUSE THEY
CHANGE THINGS. THEY INVENT. THEY IMAGINE. THEY HEAL. THEY EXPLORE.
THEY CREATE. THEY INSPIRE. THEY PUSH THE HUMAN RACE FORWARD.

MAYBE THEY HAVE TO BE CRAZY.

HOW ELSE CAN YOU STARE AT AN EMPTY CANVAS AND SEE A WORK OF
ART? OR SIT IN SILENCE AND HEAR A SONG THAT'S NEVER BEEN WRITTEN?
OR GAZE AT A RED PLANET AND SEE A LABORATORY ON WHEELS?

WE MAKE TOOLS FOR THESE KINDS OF PEOPLE.

WHILE SOME SEE THEM AS THE CRAZY ONES, WE SEE GENIUS. BECAUSE
THE PEOPLE WHO ARE CRAZY ENOUGH TO THINK THEY CAN CHANGE THE
WORLD, ARE THE ONES WHO DO."

Apple Inc.  1997

# FOREWORD: MY JOURNEY INTO HR

Like plenty of others, I ended up in human resources by accident. I worked in several different areas early in my career, dabbling in operations, sales, and IT. Then I got the opportunity to help build a department that was a hybrid of IT, operations, and quality. I loved my job, worked with a great team, and learned constantly. What more could you want?

After being in my role for a few years, I had the opportunity to join the human resources department. Our organization had a new Vice President of Human Resources (HRVP), and he asked if I would join the team and take over Human Resources Information Systems (HRIS) to help get it straightened out. I did and fell in love with HR. Over the next two years, he did more for my career than anyone else I had ever worked with. He let me spend time in talent management and acquisition, run the budget, and serve as a generalist for our corporate office, which included working directly with many of our executives. Not only did this give me a glimpse into how a public company was run, it loaded me with more HR experience than I would have imagined in a very short time.

When the time came to look for my next role, I found one that combined HR with Lean Six Sigma, which I had practiced during my earlier position. For the next three years, I spent my time on projects with significant impact on the organization, both operational and financial. HRIS implementation, self-service systems, international teams, and functional projects were all part of the experience. And I soaked up as much as I could.

During that stretch, I started writing LeanHRBlog.com. I was amazed at how many blogs were available that talked about the problems in HR and all the reasons the profession wasn't getting better. There seemed to be very few, though, that had any interest in trying to improve HR. I knew firsthand that the tools and discipline I learned working with Lean Six Sigma were not only applicable but also incredibly valuable in HR. I focused, then, on sharing the tools and how they could be applied in the transactional world.

The blog led me to make some great connections through social media and exposed me to the great writers and thinkers in the HR space. I was amazed that there was very little out there in regards to process improvement, and I learned that I was one of the very few voices in that particular lane. It took little time (and even less encouragement) for me to agree to speak on the subject, and soon I was being invited to share some of the basics around the country.

My goal in putting this book together is twofold. First, I want to share the tools and techniques I've learned for finding improvement opportunities, selecting the right projects for investing time and energy to rebuild, and managing a project portfolio to keep them all running smoothly. Second, I want to make sure my fellow HR practitioners find that this all applies to them, not just to manufacturing or supply chain. This is an arena in which we can play, and I want to share some thoughts about ways to see our world from a different angle.

I love to share what I know and also love to write, so I suppose a book on the subject was inevitable. I've certainly evangelized through every other communication channel. Sitting down to put it all in print, somehow, makes it more impactful. So what you will find in these pages will be a summary of what I've seen, what has worked, the tools that I've found extremely valuable, and a few thoughts on applying them wisely. I hope you find it helpful as you start your own improvement journey. If so, please pass it along to someone else. The HR community needs those who share their success!

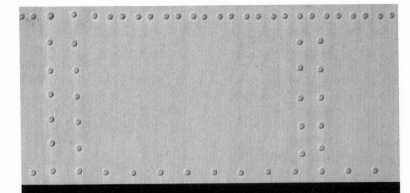

# INTRODUCTION
# WHAT IS "LEAN HR" ANYWAY?

● ● ●

This is a question I've heard more than I'd like to admit. With a number of ways it could be interpreted, it's probably worth pausing for a moment to define what it is, at least in the confines of this text.

There is an old joke among Lean practitioners (and, you should know, none of our old jokes are particularly good) that "Lean" stands for "Less Employees Are Needed." We usually only tell this joke in dark corners of the warehouse or late at night after a few adult beverages. That's because we secretly believe it may be true, especially in the transactional world.

Let's face it, most of the expense of running a business, other than manufacturing, is in salary and benefits of employees. When you are a cost center like HR, it is very difficult to generate savings, and the siren's call of employee cost is one that can be difficult to resist. But resist you must if you are to build a viable program of continuous improvement.

Over the years, "process improvement" has become synonymous with "headcount reduction." That leads to an immediate negative reaction to any changes you propose, not to mention difficulty in recruiting team members and acquiring data. From the very beginning, it will be important to shield your eyes from headcount when looking at cost savings. Not only is it dangerous long term, those savings are rarely realized as expected.

I worked with a large organization that had just completed a major acquisition, leaving them with, effectively, three distinct HRIS systems.

While these were all owned by the same parent company, the leadership team wisely used this as motivation to overhaul their platform, and convert or upgrade the entire organization into one environment.

We started with the business units based in the U.S. This was the standard implementation path, as roughly half of the employee population was U.S. based. The team completed the process review and system work in roughly a year, though the work of migrating all the employees into a common data set inside the HRIS was postponed. The second phase was to perform the same work with our European locations, which introduced the complexity of language, European labor laws, data privacy laws, and the perception that we were pushing a U.S. centric system on them. The third phase was defined as "everyone else," which is not a great choice if you are trying to keep a truly global mindset.

Phase one was an overwhelming success financially. Eliminating redundancy and streamlining operations brought back huge saving, and there was much rejoicing. As we prepared for phase two, the discussion went back to "What's the ROI?" This was a bit confusing for the team, as we had already delivered significant savings in phase one. The leadership team, though, looked at those savings and saw no connection to the cost of phase two.

Whoops.

This is a common method of calculating savings, by the way, and the leadership team had the correct approach. But the project team hadn't taken the time to fully understand the approach leadership would take, and the project champion hadn't fully communicated the expectations on both sides. The net result is that the team was asked to find savings for the next two phases of the project, most of which had been realized in phase one.

The part of the overall project that had not been implemented, even in the U.S., was employee and manager self-service. These tools are criminally underused in more businesses than you might imagine, and they were to be tackled in the near future. The hope was that the HRIS implementation would be allowed to rest, letting the HR team get comfortable with the data and system before exposing them to employees and managers directly. Suddenly, though, there was a new imperative to find savings to complete the primary project. The project leadership pushed self-service to the front, and projected savings from its implementation. Where did those savings come from?

Headcount reduction.

The team recoiled, knowing that our project just became much more difficult. Suddenly, we carried the burden of knowing we were putting our teammates out of work. Leaders from each business unit were asked to submit the names of which people could go. While we weren't exactly Lean, we had already lost headcount in previous reductions, so we looked at the people who were still left as important. And, as the faces of the project, we each knew that sooner or later we were going to have to account for the fact that our work was putting someone else out on the street.

Truthfully, this can be a great motivator to find inventive ways to improve, as well as getting a change adopted. I've had success overcoming a blocker by asking which three people from their team they would like to let go in lieu of accepting a new process. It's a sobering, but very real, conversation to have.

But if Lean HR isn't about inventive ways to get rid of your employee base, what is it? Does it mean learning to operate with a smaller HR department? Is it about making your HR team more effective at dealing with job assignments and overlap? Is the end goal to get the team to start a weight loss competition? While none of those are bad ideas, the truth is both simpler and more powerful.

Lean HR, in my opinion, is simply not doing things that don't really matter. It's about asking why a lot. It's about letting go of the things that don't make you better at what you do. And it's about the individual responsibility of people to think critically about their job and find ways to do it better. That's a key component of Lean, and you will never really create a self-propagating improvement culture without that mindset.

How do you know what matters? Spend a day asking people why they do things. I don't mean in an existential kind of way. I mean asking them about discrete tasks, big and small, and see how many people on the team really understand the work they do. They may know the immediate upstream and downstream processes, they may even be able to identify the eventual customer. But it is far too common that people operate with blinders, rarely questioning the value of their work or how to improve it. Be assured, this is a direct results of projects that eliminate headcount somewhere in their past.

A favorite fallback I hear from practitioners is that we are "legally obligated" to do certain things. While I encourage everyone to maintain a healthy respect for the law, I also suggest they take the time to find and read the statute in question. Often you will find that your "obligation" has been filtered repeatedly be others who don't understand it, and are taking their best guess at the real requirements. Taking the time to read and understand employment law, even if it means taking a member of your legal team to lunch and reviewing it with them, will make you more effective in your HR role and eliminate more process waste than you can imagine.

When you start to ask a lot of questions, be prepared to receive incomplete answers, whispered comments in the hall and, in more developed organizations, the stink eye. (If you've ever been stink-eyed, you'll know what I mean. If not, you soon will.) Humans are, by nature, keenly attuned to threats to themselves, a trait heightened in the workplace. It will take time for those around you to get used to questions, so you will need to be patient and prove that you are committed to use your powers on inquiry only for good.

As we dig into ways to uncover and investigate project-level improvement opportunities, you will need to ask questions that may seem intimidating, accusatory or inflammatory. When (not if) you are accused of being on a "witch hunt," keep smiling. Stay true to the course. Let your subject vent, then help explain the reason they are the best person to explain how their job could be improved. It will be important to help them understand the difference between investigating them and investigating the process, and that you are trying to find ways to make their work more enjoyable and productive. Admittedly, this will not always be embraced, and you may encounter those who become agitated by any implication that they aren't doing the best they could. Just remember that anger can be your best friend. When people are angry, they generally desire to see something change. Your primary task then becomes helping them pick the right thing to be changed.

We will also talk about tools that can be leveraged at the project level and the individual level. Most of these are designed to help you find the root cause of a problem, identify potential solutions or choose between options. The tools I've selected for inclusion are easy to learn, easy to use and, in most cases, require very little time or preparation to use. This is to help you as a practitioner, giving you options that can be pulled out of your toolbox at any given moment. I've had sessions where I cycled through five or six different methods of reaching an agreement, finding that the right fit was as much about the audience as the tool. Don't be afraid to try a different approach, scrap a discussion halfway through, or create a new tool on the fly. Lean isn't about sticking to the rules. Lean is about finding what works and what's really important.

It won't be easy or comfortable, in all likelihood. Starting from scratch will feel a bit like stepping onto a moving sidewalk in the airport. Personally, I love moving sidewalks. They make me feel like I'm finally living in the future that *The Jetsons* promised me. Also, I am often struck with the similarities between moving sidewalks and Lean.

Both are a different way of getting from point A to point B. Both are effective at moving a large group from A to B, but that only happens if everyone is moving. We've all seen these things jam up when one person wants to lounge on the walkway, usually on the left side (despite the multiple very clear signs to stand on the right). But when everyone is working together, it's magic.

The other similarity that I notice is when stepping onto the belt. It feels a bit wonky at first. The speed changes, the belt isn't quite as solid as the ground you were just on, and the handrail isn't always moving at the same speed as the belt. But you jump on anyway, because you've got places to go and the belt gets you there faster. Once you are on, you see all the people you are passing, even the ones who are trying really hard to prove they can move just as fast on their own. When you reach the end and step off, it's like the entire world has slowed to a crawl, and getting from point B to point C is a whole lot more work than it should be. Unless there is another moving sidewalk, of course.

So grab your bag and step on. It can be a fun ride. And if you see someone standing on the left, put your arm around them and invite them to walk with you. Or push them over the rail. With that in mind, let's take a look at how Lean evolved as a practice, and what lessons were learned that you might be able to adopt as part of your HR function.

## THE POWER OF CONTRARIAN THINKING

There has been much written about best practices and the wisdom of crowds. While you can certainly learn from other's experience, always keep in mind following the pack means you will never be in front.

There is a special power that comes from contrarian thinking, making a concerted effort to move in the opposite direction you might expect. While there are times when going with the grain makes perfect sense and is, indeed, the best answer, finding new and better ways to accomplish your task sometimes requires doing the exact opposite.

In late 2012, there was much debate over the "correct" financial policy for spurring economic growth. Jeffrey Frankel published a brilliant article, "The Procyclicalists: Fiscal Austerity vs. Stimulus," which outlined cycles of spending that trend in line with the economy. In strong periods, they emphasize spending and tax cuts. In weak, they feature spending cuts and increased taxes. While this appears to make sense, Frankel's deeper analysis shows how these cycles, especially in the U.S. over the last thirty years, may have done more damage than harm. In contrast, a review of some emerging markets that have taken a countercyclical approach reveals a period of growth in the period 2000–2010, a difficult global economic environment to say the least. While the article falls far short of overwhelming data and analysis, it does provide a fine example of the power a counterintuitive approach can yield. Frankle does, though, provide one of the best examinations of the difficult of contrarian thought I've seen.

Trying to turn left or right at precisely the wrong points in the road is a worse record than one would get by switching policies randomly. To explain this perverse pattern, let us switch metaphors mid-stream. It is the old problem of needing to fix the hole in the roof when the sun is shining, rather than waiting for a storm to realize that it is necessary. When the economy is booming, there is no political support for painful spending cuts or tax increases. After all, everything seems fine; why make a change? Then when the deluge comes, sinners suddenly see the evils of their ways and proclaim the necessity of reforming. Of course it is very difficult to fix the roof in the middle of a thunderstorm.

At it's most basic level, a contrarian hears, "You can't do that!" and thinks, "Why not?" More simple than easy, it is an approach that, with practice, may start to come very naturally.

In a project designed to make employee name changes more efficient and effective, especially in the case of marriage or divorce, an organization I worked with spent quite a bit of time looking at the legal requirements of U.S. documentation policies. After weeks of work, we identified the biggest obstacle to having identification documents (Social Security card, Driver's License, etc.) reviewed and recorded. We determined we needed to identify someone at each of our locations who was a certified Notary, who could send copies of these documents to our central team. We believed that having a list of those people would allow us to automate a message, directing the employee to the right person for submitting their documents. We looked at our systems, and determined we could easily capture Notary status as a certification with minimal setup and maintenance. It was then that our legal advisor gave her opinion that, as simple as it might seem, we weren't likely to be able to complete the task.

"You'll never get the field to keep those records up to date," we were told. Our advisor, of course, was in the right position to gauge the likelihood of success, and that may have been enough to discourage some teams.

"Why not?" I asked. (As I said, once you are accustomed to asking, it is tough to turn it off.)

"We've been down this road. There are too many people to keep track of, too many locations. You'll never have them all. We tried it once before, and were never able to pull it off." I thought about that for a moment, and responded in the only way that makes sense to a contrarian.

"Thanks for the advice, and we'd love to have your help, but we aren't ready yet to fail at something that we haven't actually tried."

Will contrarian thought always deliver success? Not at all. But it's the only way to have a chance at a big return. And it's essential to creating a Lean environment. While it can be intimidating to voice an opinion that goes against the grain, it's critical for real progress.

Along the same lines, there is sometimes a belief that Lean becomes important when an organization's performance dips. While it's never a bad time to eliminate waste, the best path is in line with Frankle's countercyclical approach. When results are good, it's time to eliminate waste.

Recently I had a discussion regarding the process improvement team's function in the organization, and their job security in a difficult economic climate. When things go south, that's when you really need your Lean leaders to help right the ship and bring savings home to maintain profitability.

I call shenanigans on that line of thought.

We need our Lean leaders to be the most engaged when times are at their best! We need to be out front, leading the discussions when people are least interested in listening.

No business I have encountered has ever said, "Nah, we don't need that $50,000. Go ahead and throw it in the trash." At least, not any that stayed around long.

While you can use the opportunity of a challenging quarter or year to "reset" your organizational perspective and drive Lean thinking, you need to do so just as hard in the good times. If not, the good times may not stay as long as you might like.

What would your company's position be today if you increased operating income five percent a year over the last ten years? Or reduced waste by twenty-five percent? Do you think you would be better positioned in the market?

Lean HR is about peering into the soul of your organization and steeling yourself to challenge what you find there. It can be ugly, scary, lonely, and unappreciated. But it can also give you a fantastic opportunity to have a real impact on your workplace.

## LEAN AND INNOVATION

One last thought before jumping in. It's not unusual to hear that pursuing Lean, with it's focus on simplicity and waste reduction, can stifle innovation. Personally, I find the idea of Lean and Innovation being bitter enemies is prevalent enough to merit some discussion.

If you think Innovation and Lean aren't chummy, you haven't spent much time in a real Lean environment. Let's think about what makes up Innovation.

- **The introduction of something new**
- **The process of creating new ideas, methods, products or services**

Pretty straightforward. Now let's think about what Lean really gets you.

- **Identify new ways of performing work with less waste**
- **Eliminate non-value added (busywork) to allow for more valued activities to be completed in less time**
- **Identify application methods to increase throughput and productivity**

Not exactly diametrically opposed ideas. Clearly, there are plenty of people who don't understand or haven't been exposed to Lean. There's a fear that Lean means layoffs, and only the bare minimum of people will be around after.

The truth is that most companies are looking to grow, not shrink. That means more people, not fewer. But to do so effectively means getting rid of the busywork and letting you focus on doing things that matter to your customers. That's how you increase your business, that's how you grow. Lean helps you find that busywork so you can eschew it.

There is also the continuous improvement side of Lean. It's not enough to just eliminate the easy to find waste. You have to look deeper and keep finding ways to go faster, safer and at higher levels of quality. To do that, you have to be creative and innovative. Just try coming up with better answers with no new ideas.

The idea that Lean and Innovation are enemies is nonsensical. Lean and Innovation are like peanut butter and jelly. Both good, but are way better together.

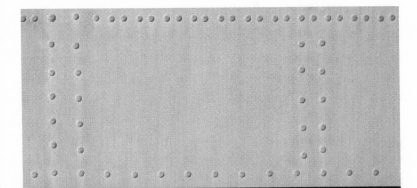

# 1
# THE EVOLUTION OF LEAN

• • •

There have been a number of different names applied to the concept of being more efficient and more productive in the business world. The term *Lean* was coined by John Krafcik in his 1988 article, "Triumph of the Lean Production System." His work at Massachusetts Institute of Technology (MIT) was the inspiration for the book *The Machine That Changed the World* by Jim Womack, Daniel Jones, and Daniel Roos. Much of this work focused on the manufacturing world, which is where Lean is most often applied.

Many people consider the Lean methodology to have been perfected at Toyota as part of their Toyota Production System (TPS). But to really understand how radical their approach to the automotive business was, you have to step back further to see from whence it came.

Early automobiles were more works of art than mass-produced goods. Due to the limitations of the time, especially that of being able to cut hardened steel with any precision, craftsmen were required to build each car by hand. Working from a general design, parts would be cut oversized and hardened, which would often warp or distort the metal. To get the pieces to fit, craftsmen would take metal files to those parts and grind away the edges until the piece met their measured specifications. It was a lot of manual labor to produce one piece of a larger project. Of course, this meant that those involved in building cars knew them intricately, and their influence of each finished product was akin to a signature at the bottom of a painting.

The industry progressed in that manner quite happily until disrupted by a young visionary named Henry Ford. You may have heard of him. Ford brought a number of notable innovations to automobile manufacturing. He set wages for workers; created the left-side steering wheel; invented an enclosed motor (although it is worth recognizing that one could be repaired by most car owners with a few simple tools); and, of course, started the assembly line. The key to mass production, though, was that the parts used for assembly were interchangeable, cut to specifications after hardening, and simple enough for any member of the team to assemble.

Of course, the law of unintended consequences controls the universe. I doubt that anyone, Ford included, had any idea how the assemble line method would impact labor for the next century. The job of each worker suddenly shifted from building a car to performing a finite task ad nauseam that, when combined, would produce a vehicle. Employees shifted from craftsman to laborer. This change would proliferate throughout business—the end result being a workforce that is task-oriented and often oblivious to the holistic nature of their work.

The next great leap forward in the automotive manufacturing world started in Japan with TPS. Essentially, the company was facing limited resources, including people, capital, and space. Its leaders knew they would need a different approach to the way they did business to be successful. The foundation was that there was no room for waste, and everyone would play a role in finding and eliminating waste wherever possible. This mindset and the tools developed to accomplish their goals are a major influence on business today. And it is the foundation upon which we shall build, leveraging them into measurable improvements in your HR practice.

Success in business is often built upon the ideas of others. While the foundation of Lean came from the automotive industry, it didn't take long for it to be adopted in other areas. Manufacturing organizations all over the world grabbed onto the ideas and tools as a life preserver, using them to restructure, recalibrate, and revive their businesses. The biggest leap, however, happened when Lean tools and methods were applied to transactional processes. In some ways manufacturing processes were relatively easy to improve. When you can see the tangible inputs and outputs as well as the manufacturing process itself, looking for waste is much easier. Of course in the transactional world, much of what is done is ethereal at best. To apply Lean in this element of business is a bit tricky at times, but because of the volume of transaction executed in a routing process, even a small change has significant ramifications. Large corporations like Honeywell and General Electric (GE) have shown that Lean can be applied across the entire organizational structure and indeed must be, if the greatest result is sought.

I bring up this history because I think it is relevant to the evolution of human resources and provides a path for the direction in which we may develop as a practice. When I think of "old school" HR, I think of those first craftsmen who knew how to build a car from the ground up. They understood the intricacies of each major component, how they all fit together, and what needed to be done to ensure smooth performance. At one point, the human resources department was tied to the members of the organization. They were known by their names and faces throughout the building. They knew which employees were expecting children, which managers couldn't be trusted with the key to the liquor cabinet, and who were the real key players. At times they even shared the task of filing the edges off of parts, or in some cases the people, until the entire unit could work together.

But in the quest for cost effectiveness, we moved away from that model and into one that divided the practice into tiers. The bottom tier, which also happens to be the biggest, is comprised of many who know little about the profession of human resources, the business they are in, or the ways and means of building a talent base. Instead, they are tasked with the work of answering phone calls and emails, filtering out the "simple" questions about benefits, vacation, and tax forms. Then they channel more complex tasks to the next level. As you move further up the pyramid, you drift away from the employee, but closer to the business strategy. In essence, the work of HR has been moved as far from the work of building strategy as possible.

All is not lost. There is hope for human resources to improve, just as Toyota improved on the Ford production model. The key concepts of open communication, root cause analysis, error proofing, eliminating waste, and cooperative relations with both customers and vendors have a place in the human resources department of today! All that is required is the willingness to learn a few new tools, ask some simple questions, commit to a structure approach to the work, and let go of the idea of "perfect."

## LEAN IN THE TRANSACTIONAL WORLD

While a more recent innovation than anything Henry Ford put together, applying Lean in areas other than manufacturing has been around for years. It's no wonder, considering that some estimates say the U.S. economy is eighty percent service organizations. Even in the traditional manufacturing world, cost of goods sold (or COGS) isn't always the largest item on the balance sheet. That would be employee costs, employees often engaged in non-manufacturing work. To get the most out of your organization, you need to excel at all facets of your business.

So how can Lean principles and tools drive out waste in the transactional world? Let's take a look at a simple example from the fast food industry and find ways to reduce the process time required to complete a simple transaction. We will skip over the "manufacturing" of the meal, and concentrate on a typical transactional process: fast food pickup. This is an example of a process that you may have experienced yourself on more than one occasion.

- Arrive at restaurant (Elapsed time – 0:00)

- Wait 5 minutes in drive-through line (Elapsed time – 5:00)

- Wait on cashier to be ready for order while cashier accepts payment from another customer (Elapsed time – 5:30)

- Place order (Elapsed time – 6:00)

- Cashier reads order back (Elapsed time – 6:30)

- Wait in line to reach drive through window (Elapsed time – 8:00)

- Pay for order (Elapsed time – 8:30)

- Receive change (Elapsed time – 9:00)

- Wait for food (Elapsed time – 11:00)

- Receive food (Elapsed time – 11:30)

- Check order; If mistake found, park, return order, wait for correction (Elapsed time – 12:00, more if mistake is found.)

Now, here's an example of a revised process with a few minor changes and the impact:

- Arrive at restaurant (Elapsed time – 0:00)

- Wait 3 minutes in drive-through line (Elapsed time – 3:00)

- Place order (Elapsed time – 3:30)

- Wait in line to reach drive through window (Elapsed time 4:30)

- Pay for order (Elapsed time – 5:00)

- Receive change (Elapsed time – 5:15)

- Move to second window (Elapsed time – 6:00)

- Receive food (Elapsed time – 6:30)

- Check order; If mistake found, park, return order, wait for correction (Elapsed time – 7:00, with fewer mistakes overall.)

Notice the overall time has been reduced from twelve minutes to seven, an improvement of more than forty percent. What is that improvement worth to the business? Intuitively we know that the improvement is significant, but the changes we suggest will have a cost to implement, so how do we quantify the value of the improvement? Here are where good metrics and valuations come into play. How much is that improvement worth?

Assuming a twelve minute cycle, you will be finishing five transactions per hour. If each transaction has an average sale total of $10, we are producing $50 of revenue per hour. Assuming twelve-hour days for a full year, that equates to $18,250 in revenue per year.

If we reduce the cycle time to seven minutes, our hourly transactions jump to just over eight. (We will round down for simplicity.) This brings our yearly revenue to $28,800, an improvement of nearly sixty percent, all captured through some minor changes to the process. Simple answers, powerful results. The times in this example are a remarkable (but realistic) scenario for the restaurant, and are intended to show how you can apply Lean thinking in the transactional world.

## CRACKING THE WIP

It will also be helpful to understand how to identify where the money in your organization is often idle. Work In Process, or WIP, is a fundamental Lean concept, a drain on precious resources, and in general may be the biggest obstacle to productivity in your business.

WIP is the queue of emails, call, requests, forms, approvals, and other assorted minutiae of your daily routine. WIP encompasses all the work that is on your plate at any given moment, regardless of how much attention you can spare. As humans, we have a limited about of GAC (give-a-crap) to go around, so we have to make decisions on the fly about how to parse it out. We also know that the more important work often gets pushed aside to deal with the loudest demands. It's suboptimal, but it's life.

Wouldn't it be nice to have a little more control? Of course it would. But to get there, you have to take a path that is a bit counterintuitive.

To make your life easier, you need to reduce the WIP. You can't control the requests for your time in most cases, but you can set up a system to control the flow of the requests. Believe it or not, doing so will help you work faster and reduce the time it takes to get to each request. Your filter will require you to do a few things.

*Define Capacity* — There are some fancy formulas you can use to calculate your optimal workload. But for the sake of simplicity, think about how many tasks you can actually do at any given time. For example, I've talked with recruiters who tell me they can work on twenty requests at a time, but more than that slows us down. This is part of that counterintuitive mindset I mentioned.

Think of your work like a highway. Plenty of research has shown that a road has a certain capacity at which it can optimally function. Adding just one more car slows everyone down. That's why you see stoplights for cars entering the highway in areas with high congestion. They are controlling the cars entering the road, which are essentially WIP. They are items in transit from point A to point B. Adding too many slows down each item.

What's your capacity? We'll talk about those formulas another time. For now, just realize you can't do everything at once, and trying to do so will hurt each and every item in queue.

*Selection Criteria* — If you can't work on everything at once, how do you know where to start? It's probably fair to say that not every request you receive is of equal value or need. Some are more time sensitive, some may have a greater impact on the organization, so may just be really difficult. It's up to you to determine how you handle each of them, and which one needs your attention.

You can't evaluate them individually to decide how to queue them, though. The moment you do so, they are WIP, which defeats the purpose. Not to mention the fact that the time you spend evaluation is waste. And that's not OK.

Instead, you need to establish selection criteria, your own personal triage unit. For a handy tool, use a tool like a Weighted Decision Matrix (which is covered in Chapter four). Build your criteria and add the weights. Don't forget to include the length of time in queue as a criteria. Otherwise there is work that might never get done, and that's not likely to make for happy customers. In the end, you should have a simple tool that will tell you which item enters your WIP next.

One more thing. People are not WIP. A customer standing at your desk can't be asked to stand to the side until you have capacity for one more thing. Lean is about providing value to your customer. They get your attention. That's why we don't run at 100% capacity. But that's another discussion as well.

*Holding Area* — So you've figured out how much you can handle, and which items you will work on next. What about the rest? Where does it go? Where is this "queue" we keep talking about?

It depends on your situation. In some cases, such as a large department with a central workload, there may be a gatekeeper who doles out work as you are ready for it. Central staffing teams can work this way with a lot of success. If you are on your own, though, you'll need to be your own gatekeeper. Of course, you'll have to do it without actually touching the request. Because that makes it WIP.

This is a great area to leverage technology to help you. Build a request or ticket system. Have an automated response system to let your requestor know you evaluate items as they come in and will add them to your workload to give them the optimal return time, and keep them updated on status. If you have your selection criteria ironed out, ask the requestor to fill in the criteria so the request can triage itself. Then take them as they come.

Yes, you'll have to look at incoming requests occasionally. But you don't need to look at each one. Use your holding area to gather them up and review them in batches.

You will be amazed, I think, at how much time you spend telling people you don't have time to get to their request right away. Building a queue that can triage itself and feed you work as you are ready for it will free up that time, and allow you to focus on the "value added" work of fulfilling those requests. By reducing the number of things you are working on, you can spend more time on the real work, complete tasks faster, clear out the queue and provide a better overall customer experience. Counterintuitive, but it works.

## SUMMARY

With a rich history on the automotive and manufacturing world, Lean concepts have moved in the transactional areas of the workplace with great success. Being a heavy transactional practice, there are great opportunities to improve the world of HR, reduce the administrative overhead, and allow more time to be spent on the critical activities around talent management, talent development, and business strategy.

Lean is not new. It is not revolutionary. It is not even particularly difficult to implement. What is required is the confidence that you can improve your business, you can make a difference, and you can create real change using common sense.

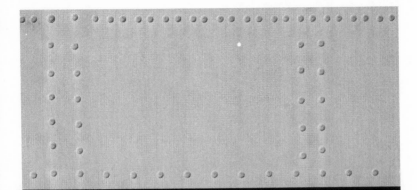

# 2

# INTRODUCING
# LEAN TO HR

● ● ●

So why does Lean matter in the HR world? Why should we worry about process improvement, waste, organizational design, and the ancillary activities those things imply?

It's no secret that all workplace organizations have been under pressure to improve performance over the last few years. With the changes in the economy and the time it has taken to start to recover, the need to reduce cost while maintaining or improving production has become nearly universal. This is especially true in staff functions like HR. As a cost center (with no reasonable expectation of producing revenue), there is not much that can be done to improve an organization's bottom line other than lowering costs. In most instances this means reducing the level of service offered to employees, decreasing the benefits they can expect from their employer, cutting headcount in the department, or some combination of those options. This runs counter to the impulses of most HR people I've met, who instinctively want to do more to help employees in tough times.

Our option, then, is to find ways of reducing the cost of HR without sacrificing benefits, quality, or people. We are left with the challenge of improving the way work is done, eliminating waste, and being as efficient as possible.

Some people will point to the recovery that has started as a signal that the pressure to improve is abating, and we can soon expect a spending binge in business not seen since the Clinton administration. I would caution them to temper those expectations. Businesses that survive tough conditions are those that can evolve and learn. What most business leaders have learned from the last decade is that they don't need to go back to higher overhead and administrative cost. They may be driving their employees harder than ever, but the work is still getting done. That's a sign that there is no need to go back to the old model, and capital can be better invested in line staff that can produce revenue.

Another impactful change in the workplace is the evolution of technology. Every day we see new products, updates to existing software, and new solutions to old challenges. Pair these with the near-constant news of mergers and acquisitions in the HR technology space, and what emerges is a constantly evolving set of tools and capabilities available to the HR department. With the amount of money spent in this area and a trend that sees it increase each year, there is ample opportunity to revisit the way we use technology. This also gives you the chance to discover overlapping capabilities and review or revise key vendor contracts to ensure you are reaping maximum value from your investment.

Finally, there is the realization that in business, revenue and profit don't always move at the same speed. Market pressures assert themselves in ways we might not expect or desire. A slew of companies have cut headcount, despite stable revenues, in an effort in improve overall financial situations. This is not to imply there is a nefarious plot afoot in those companies. Some companies make these moves to support a flagging stock price. Just as many, however, do so to stay solvent against rising expenses or ensure a credit rating that will allow continued access to capital. Regardless, these moves show just how important an efficient staff function can be. By cutting the overhead of HR or similar function, the organization can see improved finances without the need to reduce headcount. As the champions of putting people to work and keeping them there, this should be enough motivation for any HR practitioner to learn and apply a new set of skills.

To apply these concepts to an HR team that has not yet seen them will take a few preparatory measures. Aside from learning the tools and methods, you must first establish a mindset around problem solving and logical thinking. To get started, here are a few quick questions that should help shift your thinking style.

**Q: How do you put a giraffe in a refrigerator?**

**A: You open the door, insert the giraffe, and close the door.**

There's no discussion of the size of the giraffe or refrigerator in the question, which is what throws most answers. Unless we know, we shouldn't assume.

**Q: How do you put an elephant in a refrigerator?**

**A: You open the door, remove the giraffe, insert the elephant, and close the door.**

This time, we are not just assuming there's a giraffe in the refrigerator. Remember we just put one in there! Once learned, we keep information until we have good reason to acknowledge a change.

**Q: If the lion king holds an animal conference, and all animals are required to attend, who will be missing?**

**A: The elephant. He's still stuck in the refrigerator.**

This is a different question, but the fact remains that we know elephant's location from the previous answer.

Yes, these are a bit silly. Rest assured, when using Lean, incidents of stuffing wild animals in refrigerators are extremely rare. What's interesting about these questions is that young children tend to do very well with them, while adults, particularly executives, do poorly. As we age, we become conditioned to making decisions with limited information. We learn to live with our assumptions, and those that can bridge information gaps tend to rise higher in the corporate structure. Lean thinking is quite the opposite.

In Lean, we put our assumptions aside and ask for information. Asking questions can be quite daunting for some because it is essentially admitting we don't know something. While this can feel like a weakness, the truth is asking elementary questions and waiting for answers is a key skill, and is far too uncommon in today's business environment. The assumptions we make can lead to massive costs in terms of resources, money, and time.

As an example, I once worked with a team to overhaul their headcount-reporting process. Like most companies, they struggled to track headcount effectively while always believing that everyone else did so with minimal effort. On average they were spending five-person days each month to produce a complex spreadsheet; at the same time, they were desperate to free up resources to work on other things. With a five-day agenda, we started by reviewing the current state of the inputs, outputs, and processes that went into producing the report.

Through hours of my asking questions and waiting for the answers, we discovered several interesting components of their process. We found most troubling that, rather than using a template with preexisting formulas for analysis, the team would start from scratch each month to try to "avoid errors in the calculations." Once we started that discussion, we immediately knew they could make an easy improvement in this area. (It is amazing how seemingly good ideas, once spoken aloud, fall apart completely.) The most startling realization, though, came from examining the output from the customer's perspective.

At the end of this multipage report, they had made a shaded area with a few data points, all of which were pulled directly from the initial data load with no analysis or calculations. When seen next to the complex ratios and measures on the rest of the page, they were clearly out of place.

"What are these numbers for?" I asked. The team answered me with a round of silence and nervous glances.

"We don't really know."

"Then why are they included?" I asked.

"We don't really know that either. It's always been there for as long as I've run the report."

This is a classic example of someone afraid to ask a simple question and is a massive red flag in reviewing a process. My immediate reaction was to contact the customer of this report and verify the value of the information, which shocked the team.

"You can't do that!" they cried.

"Why not?"

"This report goes to the VP of Finance! You can't just call her!"

"Why? Does she not know how to use a phone?"

"Well…no, it's not that, of course. It's…well…you just can't!"

After a few more minutes of halfhearted protests, we dialed the VP's office, and lo and behold, she answered. I suppose she didn't receive many calls and was thrilled to find out the phone worked just fine. I quickly introduced myself as well as the project and the team. Then I asked for a few moments of her time, which she was happy to give. After discussing the report, the delivery method, and timing, we finally came to the output section.

"Could you please tell us if this shaded area is used for anything?"

"Oh, that's the only part I use." Her answer caused more silence and glancing about in the room, this time tinged with a bit of panic.

"So, what about the rest of the data?"

"I have no idea," she replied. "I assume it's something the HR team uses. I only need the information in the shaded box."

They spent five days each month to produce a report that literally no one needed. The team had lost hours of productivity because they feared asking a question. Opportunities to have a meaningful impact on the organization had been wasted in favor of work that added not one iota of value. Our full week agenda came to a screeching halt. The team rebuilt the report in less than an hour and then shared the results with leadership. Of course, they were thrilled with the outcome, and everyone was able to move on to more pressing issues.

Don't underestimate the impact of asking simple questions. Activities like this happen in every organization, every function, every day. Finding them is like opening up a new revenue stream for the company. And it is HR's best chance at having a meaningful impact on the bottom line.

The headcount report story is also a great example of cooperative process building, another foundational component of Lean. By involving the customer, in this case the VP of Finance, in the discussion, we quickly learned what was important and what was not. The same goes for involving suppliers in the discussion. For example, the initial data spreadsheet the HR team received included several unnecessary columns, all of which were manually entered by the HR team. By including a report writer from the IT team, those columns were quickly identified and the report was modified to eliminate them. This meant they spent less time reorganizing information, coming up with a shorter end-to-end process with fewer points of failure.

This kind of cooperative process design is critical to Lean. It can be seen in the way Toyota designs major automotive components, including transmissions, braking, and steering. By treating vendors and customers as part of the overall process, Toyota can complete a design that delivers the right value to the customer, includes the best components from the vendor, and allows their engineering teams to know early on that their design will be the right one. By doing so, they eliminate a great deal of rework and scrap in the early stages of development, helping them move new models from concept to production significantly faster than other companies. Applied to HR, this can mean a greater level of adoption for new benefits packages, more complete talent management activities, and a training platform that quickly identifies and fills the needs of the organization.

The other critical component of Lean thinking is discarding the idea of "perfect." Lean is about continuous improvement, not making one change that fixes everything. When we redesigned the headcount report, it still wasn't perfect, so we made additional changes over the next few months that improved on our work. That required the team to accept that not only could they make changes, they were expected to do so. Those in your organization that do the work know it best. The most important thing you can do is empower them (or yourself!) to find opportunities to improve and implement a solution without waiting to ask for permission. An organization that is constantly tweaking its approach, making small improvements every day and never being satisfied with the status quo, will find itself in a state of constant evolution and adaptation. The power of that kind of culture is almost immeasurable.

## SUMMARY

The strength of Lean comes from involving everyone, including customers and suppliers, in finding ways to improve. Given the pressures on HR to reduce costs and improve effectiveness, there has never been a better time to start down the path of continuous improvement. To do so will require courage to ask questions and wait for answers, challenge the status quo, and be constantly vigilant for opportunities to make large and small changes in the way we work.

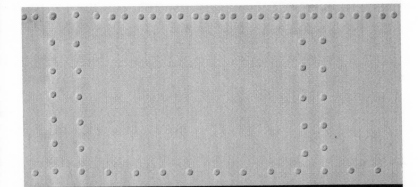

# 3
# BASICS OF LEAN

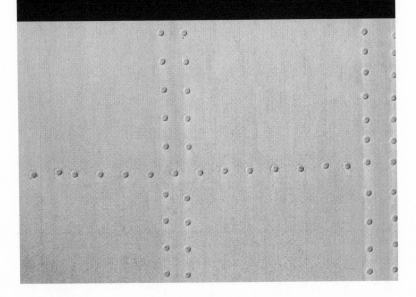

● ● ●

There are plenty of tool sets available that will help you identify and improve issues in the workplace. Most of them, I've found, are essentially the same tools under different names. With that in mind, let's review the essential components of Lean and the terms and tools you are likely to encounter.

At its core, Lean is about the identification and elimination of waste through a structured approach to problem solving. It focuses on reducing the complexity of each process and identifying areas of improvement. While the tools are not terribly complex, they do bring a level of credibility to the organization and provide the HR team a set of tools and terms that are well known by other functional leaders.

To begin, we start with the concept of value. In Lean, the customer or end user of any process defines value, and that value can best be identified by thinking in terms of billing.

As an example, let's think about the recruiting process. There are a number of steps involved in identifying a need and filling a role. While most HR teams do not invoice internal clients for the work they've done, imagine for a moment you present a detailed, itemized bill to a hiring manager for the time spent on a certain job. Your invoice would likely include the following activities: creating a requisition, getting approvals, submitting a job posting, gathering and reviewing résumés, setting up interviews, acquiring feedback, making the offer, and completing forms to move the candidate into the onboarding process. All of these are common HR activities, but let's look at them from the customer's perspective.

All the hiring manager really cares about is that you do things they can't (or don't have time to) do themselves. In that light, the activities we would consider "value added" would be sourcing candidates, interviewing them, and gaining their commitment to join. You could put these tasks on an itemized invoice and rarely need to explain.

It's also worth examining the items that aren't on that list—tasks like filling out the requisition, gathering approvals, and submitting forms for completion. While these may be important to your current process, they aren't things a manager particularly cares about in most cases. Instead they are work we would label "non-value added," or a nice way of saying "waste." It should be noted that not all waste can be avoided. Some of those activities are required for legal or corporate compliance. You may not be able to eliminate those tasks, but identifying them is the first step in improving the overall process.

The assist in determining what is value added and what is not, Lean practitioners work from a set of seven wastes. While there have been many variants over the years, these are considered the classic list.

## TRANSPORTATION

The first on this list is transportation, or the moving items from once place to another. In the manufacturing world, any setup that requires a forklift is a red flag for transportation waste. The idea factory layout would include raw material being delivered right to the first step in production and the finished product being loaded directly onto the customer delivery truck.

Manufacturing operations often work to reduce this waste by putting raw materials as close to the assembly process as possible, including putting those doing the work in close proximity. Known as workcells, the concept revolves around small groups of workers that perform discrete tasks together. For example, FIGURE 3.1 shows a traditional work setup.

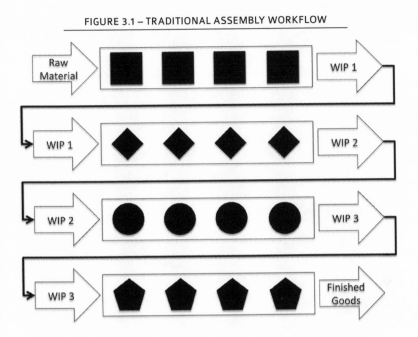

FIGURE 3.1 – TRADITIONAL ASSEMBLY WORKFLOW

The assemble steps are shape coded, and each represents a distinct change in assembly. The raw material is brought in at the start of the process, work is performed, and the work in progress (WIP) is then moved to the next step. Looking at the space between the work group and the distance the WIP must move through the assembly process, it is easy to identify the transportation waste.

Compare this to the process outlined in FIGURE 3.2, in which workcells are deployed to reduce the distance over which materials must move. The assembly steps are represented by the same shapes as in FIGURE 3.1 but are deployed to reduce total distance traveled.

FIGURE 3.2 – WORKCELL ASSEMBLY WORKFLOW

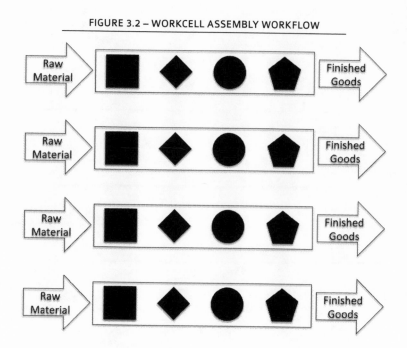

Raw materials are divided up into smaller batches, and each group produced a finished product with a greatly reduced amount of overall transportation of materials.

Transactional transportation can be a bit more ethereal, but it is no less prevalent. Think of the number of documents that pass back and forth through email in an effort to collaborate with others. Or ponder the number of phone calls you need to make to obtain one piece of information. Chasing information is certainly waste, and once you start paying attention to it, it will become readily apparent in your workplace.

### INVENTORY

The phrase "inventory is death" has been attributed to numerous sources, but the veracity of it is unquestioned. Walking through a warehouse of raw materials, finished goods, or work in progress will overwhelm a Lean practitioner. He or she will begin mentally calculating the recourses tied up in those goods, in the shelves that hold them, in the building that houses them, in the staff that counts them, and in the inevitable misplaced or obsolete items.

In the office, inventory can still be tangible, such as office supplies, furniture, or office space in general. It can also be informational inventory, such as unqualified candidates in an applicant tracking system or a backlog of unread emails. This electronic clutter will slow down anyone who needs to access information quickly, but it also has genuine cost in server space, electricity, and backup resources.

## MOTION

The waste of motion is classically defined as reaching, stretching, leaning, or walking from place to place in order to complete a task. This is traditionally associated with workspace layout, accessible materials, and proximity to suppliers and customers of each process step.

We commonly measure the amount of motion in a process through a spaghetti diagram — a visual map created through observation. As an example, FIGURE 3.3 shows a diagram that has been created of a doctor's office. Notice the location of the front desk, waiting room, supplies, and examination rooms. The lines on the graph represent the paths walked by the lead nurse as she retrieves a patient from the waiting room, takes him or her to the scales, and escorts the individual to an exam room. An additional set shows the movement to retrieve supplies from the central storage area for each patient. Taken together, the time and distance invested in this arrangement adds up to a significant amount of motion that can be eliminated through simple office redesign.

Compare FIGURE 3.3 to FIGURE 3.4, in which the central storage area has been eliminated in favor of smaller supply cabinets in each exam room. Keeping these items closer to where they will be needed (known as POUS, or Point of Use Storage) significantly reduces the distance traveled. Couple this change with focusing on using the rooms closer to the workspace, and you can see a significant reduction in motion.

The same effect can be achieved in the office by decentralizing functional groups and moving the HR team into their customers' space. This offers the additional value of being embedded within those client groups, which can improve communication and service levels.

**FIGURE 3.3 – INITIAL DOCTOR'S OFFICE LAYOUT**

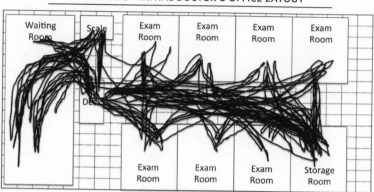

**FIGURE 3.4 – REVISED DOCTOR'S OFFICE LAYOUT**

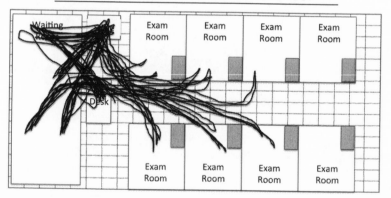

## WAITING

Nothing is as wasteful as an idle person or piece of equipment. When redesigning a process, one of the first things a Lean practitioner will look for are pieces of the process that cause one resource to wait for another. And the most common cause of that waiting — especially in the transactional world—is the need for an approval.

One of the fundamental truths in Lean is that any approval is a waste. You may not be able to eliminate all of them due to regulatory requirements, but you should be examining every one of them to be sure. And then you should design your processes to eliminate them whenever possible. To do so, first look at the design of the system leading to the approval step. Often, this involves compensation or spending. For example, anyone who has been part of making an offer to a candidate, whether internal or external, has certainly gone through an approval process with the compensation team. In most of those cases, job grades and salaries are predefined for the position. As long as the offer is within those bounds, why do you need an approval? Usually, the approval is needed because there is nothing in the process that enforces the parameters, and the person making the offer could conceivably offer far more (or far less) than the position prescribes. If the process, by design, enforced the established parameters, no further review would be required.

Sometimes waiting is part of the process. For example, any assembly using glue will require drying time. Likewise, internal review periods for policy changes may have a built-in waiting period to allow all concerned parties time for discussion. In those cases, the waiting is considered "required waste."

**OVERPRODUCTION**

The flipside of inventory is overproduction, or creating more finished goods than needed. When the amount of effort required is combined with the materials used, overproduction becomes very costly for an organization. Those that tend to overproduce often do so to compensate for a long production process, meaning they cannot quickly adapt to changes in the market or in customer demands.

While this may not seem like a common problem, you probably only need to look back to your last staff meeting to see it in action. We often consider it a courtesy to provide an agenda and printed handouts for meeting attendees, and the "just-in-case" mentality commonly causes us to produce more copies than expected attendees. This, combined with the proclivity of many to decline a set of copies, means we are left with a few unnecessary copies after the session. Each copy costs the organization in several ways, including paper and ink. The same can be said for the extra donuts provided by the catering staff, though they are usually snapped up if left in the break room (so those my not count).

## OVERPROCESSING

Part of successfully delivering on customer's needs is understanding their specifications. Overprocessing refers to the practice of not just meeting, but exceeding, those needs in a way that does not add value. The automotive industry is notorious for this, producing vehicles en masse, and then attempting to sell them to consumers who often have no need for a power moonroof or sliding rear hubcaps. Part of this is due to the business model of having production disconnected from the buyer. But it also helps in selling at a higher price, due to a lack of inventory that meets the buyer's specific desires.

Most companies will find overprocessing waste in their data and metrics reporting. Too many companies don't spend enough time thinking about their metrics and the behaviors they are trying to support. Instead they continue to track and report metrics that were once important. The best way to find waste in that area is to look critically at your reported metrics and ask yourself what action you would take if any one of the numbers doubled or was cut in half. If the answer is none, you are wasting your time tracking it.

## DEFECTS

The most obvious waste is a defect, or any good or service produced that doesn't meet the stated specification of the customer. Incorrectly reporting metrics, vehicles missing a bumper, pizza missing the pepperoni, or making an offer to the wrong candidate are all defects. Each one can be incredibly costly in business.

In Henry Ford's manufacturing plant, they set aside a staging area for completed vehicles with defects. Timing of the assembly line did not allow for the immediate correction of a mistake, so these defective automobiles were set aside until they could be repaired. This, of course, required additional resources, including staff to make the repairs and the footage used for storage. Contrast this with the Toyota assembly plant's use of andon cords, which are available for anyone to use. Pulling this cord stops the assembly line when a defect is detected. The team quickly gathers to review the cause of the defect and puts a solution in place to prevent it from happening. While time is lost to the defect, the team's focus is to make sure it only happens once, meaning fewer wasted resources long term.

You likely have defects in your workplace. The key to improving performance isn't working around defects but instead accepting that they are signs of a flawed process. Take the time to pull the andon cord in your office and share those defects with your team. Working together will help you discover ways to improve your design to not only reduce the defect, but find new ways to reduce other kinds of waste and become more effective overall.

## VARIATIONS

Many organizations, not to mention a few consultants, have modified this list to some extent. Perhaps they have renamed, or even replaced, a few of the classic wastes. The most common change is to include an eighth waste that captures unused people or underused creativity. I haven't included them in this list because those are really signs of a culture that has not embraced continuous improvement or has failed to empower people to make changes. When the environment welcomes change for the better, the chances of getting the most out of your team increase significantly.

## SIX SIGMA

It is common to find Lean and Six Sigma used together. While it can be intimidating thanks to complex mathematics and tools, Six Sigma can be a powerful ally to the Lean practitioner. While we won't go into Six Sigma in depth in this book, it might be helpful to understand how they work together.

Six Sigma is concerned with making each process repeatable, allowing for as little variation as possible. While Lean asks for customer specifications for a process output, Six Sigma looks for the upper and lower limits on those specifications. Then it tries to stay within those bounds as often as possible.

Through the use of Six Sigma methodology, the elements of the process that cause variation are found and controlled, allowing for the output of the total process to be as similar each time as possible. It also allows you to determine how much of the change in the output is due to random variation and when you should be concerned with the output moving into the range of a defect.

When used together, Six Sigma reduces the process variation, and Lean makes it more efficient by removing the process waste. The end result is a process that meets the customer specifications with the lowest possible cost to your organization. While we will focus on Lean thinking, we will leverage the Six Sigma project organizational tools in a later chapter.

## THE PROCESS EQUATION

One more concept that you need to understand before moving on is the process equation. This simple formula is a critical part of the foundation for the work that follows:

$$Y = f(X)$$

While not terribly complex, the process equation may require some explanation on first viewing. Y represents the output of any given process. X represents the inputs that are required to produce the output. And f, the function, is the way in which all the inputs combine to create the output. It may be simple, but in fact it is deceptively powerful.

Everything in life is an output. Your health, your family, your work, and your goals are all outputs. When you set your improvement goals, you are determining what your target outputs will be from those processes. Because the goals can be very high level or complex, the next step is to identify the Xs in your equation. Then you focus your time measuring and evaluating the important Xs (which are, of course, outputs from some other process themselves). But is it important to realize that if the Xs don't change, the Ys will never move—no matter how badly you want or need them to. Hope is not a strategy.

## WIP AND LITTLE'S LAW

Play around with Lean long enough, and eventually someone will ask you to do math. It's ok. You can handle it, I promise. This is one of the tools that requires calculations, but once reviewed, you'll be able to do it in your sleep.

Because Lean is about reducing waste, increasing speed and efficiency, the end result should be faster completion of tasks. How do you know if it is working? Well, you measure it, of course. In the manufacturing world, you can grab a stopwatch, walk the line, and see how long it took to produce a particular widget. Excellent. The transactional world is a bit different, though. That's where Little's Law can help. Here's the formula:

$$\text{Lead Time} = \frac{\text{Amount of WIP (Work in Process)}}{\text{Average Completion Rate}}$$

Let's break that down, shall we?

*Lead Time* — The answer to the "how long does it take?" question. This is the metric we want to drive down. You may also see this called "Takt Time." It tells your client how long they should expect to wait between submission and fulfillment.

*Amount of WIP* — The number of items on which you are working. Any task you have touched is WIP, as we already know.

*Average Completion Rate* — How many of these tasks did you complete in a day/week/month/year. A simple counting exercise. You may not know how long it really takes you to complete a talent development session, but you probably know how many you did last week.

Nothing too scary here, I hope. So what does it mean? First, if gives you a solid foundation on which you can start to calculate how long those tasks actually take. Second, it tells us that to improve your cycle time, you have to either increase the completion rate or reduce the WIP. If we think in terms of the Process Equation, you'll know that we aren't likely to change the completion rate (the Y in this case) without changing something about the steps in the work (the set of Xs). That takes time. But the WIP is totally in our control, as we have discussed.

It's worth noting that your cycle time starts when any given request enters WIP. Work in the holding queue isn't WIP, so the clock starts when you touch the request. Some may feel this isn't an accurate measure. If I don't count the time a request waits for me to work on it, of course I'll finish it in less time. Absolutely true. And you'll do it in such a way that you free up the time you spent trying stay organized, and you can focus on production. That time adds up to more work completed, which also drives down cycle time.

This will require you to create a baseline cycle time based on your WIP capacity. Otherwise, you will be comparing an unlimited WIP to a limited one, which are not the same thing. Don't get caught up in that. Lean Accounting goes through the same thing when first starting. You are changing your measurement system and your work system. You can't compare the old system to the new one with metrics that only apply to one of them. Try, and you'll get some messy, misleading data.

You have to change your way of thinking, and start measuring differently. I promise you though, you'll see a difference as you use the WIP queue and measure your cycle time consistently. Get your quick wins here, then start pulling apart the Xs of your Average Completion Rate. This is a great tool to help you understand your workload and get it under control. And remember, measuring your cycle time isn't just a good idea.

It's the law.

## SUMMARY

Lean is focused on reducing process, commonly identified as transportation, inventory, motion, waiting, overproduction, overprocessing, and defects. By being aware of these types of waste, it will be far easier to find and eliminate waste in the workplace.

Six Sigma is a toolset focused on reducing and explaining process variation. When used with Lean, Six Sigma helps to reduce random waste in the process and create a consistently high performance. Six Sigma also offers a method of organizing projects, which we will review in a later chapter, along with a few basics of statistical measures.

The most important thing to remember is that changing the outcome of a process means changing the inputs. Without meaningful change at that level, your project is doomed to failure.

# 4

# IDENTIFYING IMPROVEMENT OPPORTUNITIES

• • •

The most difficult part of any Lean transformation is getting started. Finding the right place to invest your resources is critical in the early stages to build momentum and secure additional resources for later opportunities. This can be especially difficult in overworked organizations that do not have people to assign to project-only roles. For practitioners, there seems to be a maximum of about twenty percent of their time being spent on project work before their service levels begin to suffer noticeably. For that reason, it is important to deploy those resources in ways that are not just meaningful, but also that could free up additional resources when moving forward.

There are several viable sources for project ideas, all of which are equally important in determining your improvement options.

## TOP-DOWN

Ideas that are considered "top-down" are those that are derived from the business strategy or operating plan. Sadly, far too few HR professionals have taken the time to read—let alone understand—their organization's business plan, begging the question of how fit they could be to develop the talent needed to make those plans a reality.

This commonly leads to a misalignment, either real or perceived, between an organization's plan and the HR departmental goals. This can create conflict, poorly leveraged resources, ineffective projects, or worst of all, a lack of credibility with the executive team. Rectifying this situation begins with investing the time to understand the overall direction and then determining what the HR team should be doing to support those high-level goals.

The best tool for this job happens to be incredibly simple and is really nothing more than a way to structure your thought process. It is called a Y to X Tree, and it derives its structure from the process equation. FIGURE 4.1 is an example of a Y to X tree that has been completed.

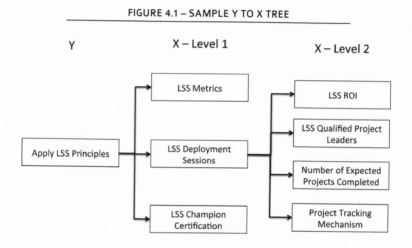

**FIGURE 4.1 – SAMPLE Y TO X TREE**

In this example, the Y is "Apply Lean Six Sigma (LSS) Principles." This is not an uncommon target for organizations that are beginning their transformational journey. As you might imagine, however, this target is far too complex to accomplish directly. Using the Y to X Tree allows us to begin to break down that high-level strategic goal into manageable chunks. Above, we have identified three major components to the initial goal: LSS Metrics, LSS Deployment Sessions, and LSS Champion Certification. While these are more distinct goals, they are still considerably complex. Because we know each X in the process equation is also a Y in its own right, we can then split each of them into smaller Xs. In this example, we focus on the LSS Deployment Session, or the way in which we will determine on which projects to work and how to manage them. We distill this into several more Xs: LSS Return on Investment (ROI), specifically the expected level of return required from a project before resources would be assigned; LSS Qualified Project Leaders (determining the level and number of project leaders that would likely be needed overall); Number of Expected Projects Completed (the expectation for each department, project leader, or team member); and Project Tracking Mechanism (determine the method and management of the data).

These Xs are all manageable goals and can be either assigned to an owner for completion or decided by leadership. In a few short steps, the Y to X Tree has moved us from high-level strategy to tactical plan and can be used to help explain the genesis of activity derived from the overall plan. You'll not only be better aligned to the holistic goals of the organization this way, but you'll also be well prepared when asked to explain the activities of your HR team.

## BOTTOM-UP

These ideas are generated from the employees of an organization, whether they are part of the HR team or another functional group. Despite the moniker, "bottom-up" ideas are no less important than top-down ideas. In fact, they are more likely to address issues that your organization is facing each day in the course of normal activities.

Gathering these ideas requires the mindset of continuous improvement that we discussed earlier. It requires an open approach to improvement, a willingness to listen, and the ability accept input from multiple sources as equally valid. Finding ways to gather this feedback isn't always easy, but there are a few ways you can encourage employees to open up about areas that need improvement.

## TEAM MEETINGS

We have all cursed the regular staff gathers as a waste of time at some point. And very often it is true waste. Information that could easily be distributed via email or by memo is instead read to the team with little or no chance for discussion. You have the opportunity to turn these sessions into valuable discussion simply by dedicating part of each meeting to planned problem solving.

Most team meetings will include at least a few moments of disgruntled comments from attendees. There's no reason that couldn't be added to the agenda as time to discuss what is keeping the team from being more productive. If you are not in a position to influence the agenda, you can still pull the discussion to the forefront with a well timed, "I'd like to talk a little about a problem I keep seeing" comment. Most leaders are more than willing to accept productive conversation in this vein, and bringing up an issue with a willingness to try to solve it will take you far.

There is a concept in Lean known as "going to the Gemba." Gemba refers to the area in which work is done. Going to the Gemba is the practice of spending time with those that are doing the work in order to understand how to improve it. This can be as simple as asking in your team sessions what needs to be done, or it can be a bit more involved. One of the classic tools used for this end is called a "Gemba circle." In its traditional application, the leader goes to a spot in the manufacturing plant or office, draws a circle on the floor in chalk (in theory, anyway, though many skip this step in favor of bringing a chair), and then stays that circle for a set length of time—often a full eight-hour workday. During that time, they observe and note any of the seven wastes they see, and those notes become the foundation of the next set of improvement goals.

The next iteration of this concept is the "Gemba walk," which is more useful in the transactional world. Process observers follow a set path each day, which follows the major steps in an activity, especially one that moves between people or departments. Along the way, interviews are conducted with those who are involved in the process execution. Not only does this allow a richer understanding of the process than can be gleaned from a map, but it also helps discover connections and unintended consequences that have a significant impact on the process outcome.

As an example, I was able to participate in a Gemba walk program at a hospital, specifically looking at their surgical area. We started with the scheduling assistant, moved through the pre-operation area, onto the surgical unit, and finally to post-operation and discharge. While the walk was very informative—both for the level of detail in the process and the quality of care being provided—there were noticeable dips in productivity. Part of our task was to understand why.

In healthcare the metric labor per stat (LPS) dictates much of how the workforce is deployed. The concept measures how many labor hours are spent for each distinct process, service, or operation. This means that when the number goes up, the administration works to reduce the hours spent, often resulting in cutting back the schedule or asking staff to use vacation hours. In this particular Gemba walk, we saw that the scheduling assistant was one of the first to go, as she was neither involved in direct care nor was she considered a critical member of the staff.

As we walked through the process and found productivity sags, we were able to correlate them to the reduction of the scheduling assistant's hours. At first glance, it would make sense that there is a correlation between the two, but we soon found it was actually a causal relationship. The scheduling assistant's role was to coordinate with external doctors to ensure surgical patients were on the schedule, were aware of their appointments, had their correct paperwork, and that the information and approvals from those doctors were received prior to the patient's arrival. Reducing her hours meant the process was not as well prepared, appointments were missed, paperwork was incomplete, and patient satisfaction dipped.

This connection, which is blindingly obvious in hindsight, was not discovered until the Gemba walk offered a holistic view of the process. Until you have a full view of the upstream Xs and downstream Ys of your process, you will never really understand where they are and how to improve them.

## SURVEYS

I will be the first to admit I hate surveys with the heat of a thousand suns. That's mostly attributable to their poor deployment, though, and not to the tool itself. If properly leveraged, surveys can give you a tremendous amount of information in exchange for very little effort. If poorly deployed, they can seriously impact your team's credibility with your employees.

I once had a conversation about an employee survey with someone from another organization.

"I just resent that I'm forced to fill this out each year. No one reads it anyway." Upon hearing this, the HR person in me stepped up to be part of the discussion.

"Of course they read it! A tremendous amount of resources and money are dedicated to this process each year! Your feedback is really important, and this is really the only way to capture it."

"Well, it's not really anonymous. I can tell by the questions they ask."

"Usually it's compiled by a third party, so there's not really much that can be traced back," I said. "But the demographics are useful to figure out some of the underlying information."

"If they really cared about feedback, they wouldn't have just done multiple choice questions. They'd let us tell them what we really think instead of picking from their answers." The data guy inside heard this and felt the need to speak up.

"Do you have any idea how long that would take to analyze? You have 60,000 employees in your company. Text answers would take a full year just to read through," I said.

"WHY ARE YOU TAKING THEIR SIDE?!?" came the response, along with fire being shot from her eyes. I backed slowly away and made a mental note to avoid discussions about employee surveys if at all possible.

The truth is people dislike completing surveys because, in most cases, there is no payback. Their responses are rolled in with thousands of others, and little or no action is ever taken, at least from their perspective. For that reason, it is difficult to leverage the tool to any significant extent. There are a few things you can do to make it a useful feedback option, however.

First, keep your surveys simple. Shoot for five questions, which will limit the time it takes to complete. Keep your response scale to either three or four, so it is easy to answer. Responding to a three-point scale is extremely easy. Agree, neutral, or disagree. Above average, average, or below average. Exceeded expectations, met expectations, or below expectations. A four-point scale forces the user to choose a side on the positive/negative prism, with no neutral answer allowed. Strongly agree, slightly agree, slightly disagree, or strongly disagree. Regardless of your question, one of these two scales will do the job. No additional complexity is required, and if included, it will often obfuscate your results.

## OUTSIDE IN

There is tremendous potential for discovering improvement opportunities outside of your organization. While much of the social media push of the last few years has implored professionals to network, there is rarely anything said about the purpose of that networking. Here is the value you can capture from those activities.

It is exceedingly rare to encounter a problem or an idea that is entirely unique to your organization, and there is no need to believe that you must solve problems in a vacuum. By leveraging the power of social tools and creating an ever-widening circle of references, you will have access to the collective wisdom and experience available in the business world. Time that was once spent creating policies, guidelines, and tools from scratch can now be better spent asking for examples and then adapting them to your own situation.

The power in this approach lies in the correct adaptation. Too often in business we hear about "best practices," which are often dropped into a situation with little thought as to how well they will fit the need, culture, and opportunity. In many ways, it's the same difference as between a cover and a copy in the music world.

I love Cake. And while that is true in many different ways, I'm not speaking today about the icing-delivery system we all know so well. Instead I'm referring to the band whose most popular song, "Short Skirt, Long Jacket." You've probably never heard of it. What is really interesting, though, is their selection of cover songs across their albums. "War Pigs" (yes, the old Black Sabbath song); "Ruby" (yes, the old Kenny Rogers song); "I Will Survive" (yes, the old Gloria Gaynor song); and "Mahna Mahna" (yes, the old Muppets song) are all served up in new ways.

Cover songs aren't easy to pull off. If you start with a great tune, you can either try to copy the original or do something new with it. If the tune is weak, you have to save it from itself. A cover implies you do something new, so a lot of respect is due for a band like Cake (as well as Alabama 3 and the White Stripes) for doing new things with good material. The Stripes get extra credit for taking material that would be considered weak by the current audience (Dolly Parton's "Jolene," for instance) and making it popular. In a few cases, the cover is considered highly superior to the original.

All of this is an interesting way to look at best practices. The key to leveraging a best practice from someone else is to cover it, not copy it. It's not likely that your practice is identical to anyone else's, so you probably can't just create a carbon copy of someone else's process and use it successfully. Your organization needs the results and the great ideas that are out there, but your talent and knowledge are just as important.

As an example, I've worked with organizations that were great at talent acquisition. We put together a very comprehensive program of SLAs, documents, résumé filters, processes, transfer maps, and rules. We reduced cycle time and implemented some great metrics and governance models that you wouldn't believe. It was important for a large organization with a lot of talent to watch over. I think it was a highly successful program that improved our operation across the board. Does that make it right for you? Maybe, maybe not. But you certainly wouldn't be able to take our documentation and use it as written.

Another fine example is the work Melissa Mayer undertook immediately after taking the CEO role at Yahoo! Within the first two weeks, she had instituted many of the programs and benefits popular at her former employer, Google. While only on the first wave of change she expected to implement, the company was more than a little criticism of her attempts to "Googlize" the environment, rather than develop it organically. While her long-term success will take some time to evaluate, it's no mystery that taking a best practice shortcut opens you up to criticism for being shortsighted and unimaginative.

Your organization may not need a massive overhaul. Maybe you just need a clean recruiting plan template. Maybe you need a way to communicate your progress to your hiring managers. Maybe you need to outsource your recruiting and focus on your retention efforts. Maybe you really do need free lunches and backrubs. It all depends on your organization. Are there elements you can lift and shift? Probably. The best way to find out is to dig into the best practices you find, really understand them, and then find the parts that will resonate with your customers. The rest is waste.

Take the time to understand the harmony, the melody, the bass line, and the groove of those best practice and bend them into your own songs. Cover. Don't copy.

The corollary, of course, is that you may have experience with a problem someone else is facing. You owe it to your peers and fellow practitioners to make yourself and your knowledge available to them as well. The community needs those who put themselves at the disposal of others to move forward. Don't be shy.

Gathering all these ideas will be an ongoing project, as will managing them and making sure you are deploying your resources properly. Don't underestimate the amount of work that will go into the management of your idea and project portfolio. It will be significant.

## BRAINSTORMING TOOLS

Whether you are looking at top-down, bottom-up or outside-in sources for improvements, at some point you will need to actually think about what you can improve. You will someday find yourself in a room with a team, I'm sure, searching either for the next great project or the solution to the world's toughest problem. Finding ways to help your team be creative is a critical skill.

While I am partial to structured thinking and methodical project generations, there is great potential in free form thinking. But don't mistake "free form" for "completely unstructured." Not many great ideas come out of a room full of people staring at their navels. You can use well-established tools and methods for free form idea generation. In fact, great brainstorming sessions have a few common traits.

- **A defined time limit. Without this, you can go spiraling off into the void. A time limit will keep you focused.**

- **A defined problem to be solved or goal to be reached.**

- A method of recording results. Sticky notes work great. I'm also a fan of whiteboards, depending on the method being used.

- Someone assigned as facilitator to drive the exercise and make sure time is productive.

There are many different methods you can use. Here are a few examples to get you started...

*Y to X trees* — We've covered these already, but they have great potential as idea generators. Don't forget them.

*Worst Idea* — This method starts with someone, usually the facilitator, throwing out the worst solution to a problem they can think of. For example, if you are looking to reduce the cost of labor, fire all employees and replace them with robot monkeys. Robot monkeys powered by hugs. Bad idea, indeed. But hearing bad ideas can often stimulate our minds to think of incrementally better ideas, and get the creative juices flowing.

*Back to Front* — A reverse Y to X Tree, in some ways. Start with your end state, take each attribute of your desired outcome, and drive backwards to the source. If your outcome is sweet, tasty sausage, you can define the components (casing, meat, spices, etc.) and then determine the best source for each. The answers you find might be very different than how you currently start a process.

*Six Hats* — In this exercise, participants are assigned a specific colored hat. Props are most certainly appropriate. Each hat represents a way of thinking about the problem. The real power of this method is when the participants begin to feed off of each other, not just thinking in isolation.

- **WHITE – ANALYTIC: Considers only "known" facts.**

- **RED – EMOTIONS: Focuses on instinct and emotional reactions to problems.**

- **BLACK – OBSTACLES: Seeks and calls out roadblocks to success.**

- **YELLOW – BENEFITS: Looks for opportunities to gain more from a solution, focused on the common good.**

- **GREEN – CREATIVITY:** Attempts to get teammates to think in new ways or areas within their color.

- **BLUE – META:** Often the facilitator, this person focuses on the thinking process.

There are plenty of other methods out there that work, but these are some of my favorites. In the end, whatever tool gets your team moving is the right one to use.

## THE KANO MODEL

One other thing to consider as you seek out improvements is that, realistically, not every improvement is worth pursuing. While your fiscal targets for waste reduction will drive some of your decisions, you should also consider the value of investing your resources. The Kano Model is a tool that may be of assistance in this process.

Once upon a time there was a wise man named Noriaki Kano. He developed the model you see in FIGURE 4.2 to explain different dimensions of customer value. Let's take a look at the basics of this model and how it works.

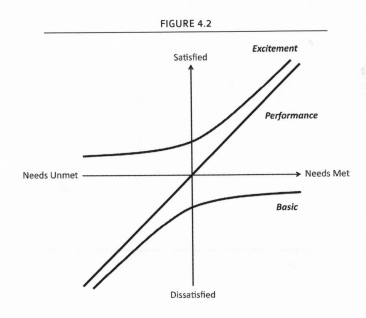

FIGURE 4.2

*The horizontal axis is the measure of need fulfillment. We move from the need being unmet on the left to the need being fulfilled on the right.*

*The vertical axis is a measure of customer satisfaction.*

*The three diagonal lines are representation of types of transactions or services.*

*Excitement:* Also known as "delighters," these activities generate a high response from users once a certain level of performance is achieved, but below that level there is not much return for the effort. In other words, meeting the basic need of the user generated little more response than ignoring that need completely. They can be ignored with very little impact, but providing them makes the difference in customer satisfaction.

If you attend a movie in a theater, you have expectations of the screen, the sound, the popcorn and the soft drinks. But what if the theater also provided additional amenities, like a private lounge for the screening, or a selection of alcoholic beverages? These are not the normal experience, and the their lack of availability are not likely to cause you to feel dissatisfied. Providing them, though, can turn an average movie experience into a memorable night and drive return business. This group is where innovation really drives performance. Don't forget, though, that these "delighters" can quickly become commodities that turn into expectations, driving them into the "basics" area. (Imagine a theater that didn't sell concessions!)

*Performance:* The classic intersection of performance and reward. The better you perform, the more it is appreciated. A great example of this is a purely price driven market. The lower the price of a commodity, the higher expected user satisfaction will be. When the price of gas goes up, our satisfaction goes down. When it goes down, our satisfaction rises. This assumes, of course, you are the consumer and not the president or shareholder in a major refining company. In that case, the line would still likely be the same, but the needs and satisfaction ratings viewed a bit differently.

*Basic:* This activity type generates great levels of dissatisfaction if not fulfilled, but very few bonus points are awarded for excellence. Most of us own toasters. They make toast. And as long as it makes toast when asked, it generally doesn't get a lot of attention. A slightly faster toaster? Yawn. Available in many colors? Great, thanks. Upgraded timer feature? Hand crafted outer casing? Aerodynamic plunger? Not likely to get anyone excited. As long as our bread gets toasted, we don't get think too much about the extra functions of the toaster.

## PUTTING KANO MODELS TO WORK

How many times have you or your peers tried to deploy a new process or tool, only to have it met with a "meh" from your clients? When you KNOW it's a quality product and that it works as designed, your frustration can skyrocket and your motivation disappear. Why does it happen, and why does it get us down?

Well, the second part is easy to answer. We're humans. (Most of us, anyway.) We like to be successful, we like to be recognized and appreciated for what we bring to the table. And when our projects aren't met with much fanfare, it stings.

More important, though, is why they are met with anything less than ticker tape. Think back to the last time this happened. Examine the process or tool, and think about where it falls on the Kano model. There are real dangers of non-acceptance for each category.

The strength of the model is in helping you develop strategy and target your efforts in a way that will increase customer satisfaction. You can be sure that world class companies spend their time innovating theater experience, not redesigning toaster plungers.

One of the benefits of the tool is that you don't need hard data to use a Kano Model. These are intuitive discussions on the things you do in your normal business activities. In the HR world, where data can be so difficult to obtain, these types of tools are too valuable to be ignored. As an example, let's take a look at the following services and processes in the compensation world:

- **Setting salary and bonus targets**
- **Benchmarking competitive compensation structures**

- Managing corporate balanced scorecard

- Paying performance bonuses

Let's break these down into the three Kano categories. These are my opinions based on experience, though your particular experience may be different.

### Basic

*Setting salary and bonus targets* — Managers and employees rarely want a new and exciting way of getting this data, or new ways to look at your targets. They generally want to see the targets so they have an anchor point for conversations and comparisons.

*Benchmarking competitive compensation structures* — Generally benchmarking is a snapshot, or multiple snapshots over time, based on criteria that are hopefully derived from your strategy. Delivering the results of benchmarking is more about understanding how you compare to others, so you are by nature somewhat restrained in innovation. If you get too innovative, after all, there may not be a benchmark. A good problem to have, but it takes you in another direction.

*Paying performance bonuses* — Much like any payroll function, this is an area where execution is critical, but innovation is less sought after.

### Excitement

*Managing corporate balanced scorecard* – OK, "managing" a scorecard could be seen as a Basic function. But I'm going to assume that part of management of the tool is changing or enhancing that tool as well. Looking for new ways to measure how we perform, teasing out correlations and metrics in a transactional world, and relating those back to hard business results can uncover interesting and valuable data. (Admittedly, it may not be exciting to everyone, but it is to some.)

### Performance

Nothing on this list, I would say, falls into the Performance range. No surprise, as compensation is an area that must perform at certain levels, but doesn't normally become a differentiator for employees, with the notable exception of the size of the check.

*Basic* tasks should, in general, be developed until they reach the satisfaction stage, and then either left alone or centralized/automated/outsourced. When you only have to be "good enough" there is no reason to spend more effort there. So stop. (Note: "Good enough" will vary on the task, naturally. For payroll, "good enough" may be "error free." Don't assume "good enough" is a half-hearted effort.)

*Excitement and Performance* tasks are where differences are made. They should take up the biggest part of your attention. The better you get at them, the more value they return to you and, more importantly, your customers.

*Excitement* items will get people, well, excited, but only if you execute them at a high level. Rolling out a first pass or draft version that isn't spot on and error free will actually hurt your credibility. People don't want early iterations. They want final products. These projects are the ones that should come with a warning tag to ignore due dates, and focus on a deliverable list instead.

A whole different approach applies for Performance tasks. These are the projects that do benefit from iterations. We like gas at $1 per gallon, and we like it a whole lot more than gas at $3 per gallon, but we still buy it at $3 because we need it. Buying expensive gas is, in most cases, less painful than not buying gas at all.

If you are building a *Performance* tool (such as a self service system), you might be well suited to roll out a stripped down basic version first, building momentum and credibility, and then cycling through iterations of improvements. As long as each version brings more value to your customers, your adoption rate and positive feedback will increase as well.

The key to successful project implementation is knowing when to release and when to delay. Knowing where your project falls in the Kano can help you time your activities to get the most out of your work and position it for the best response from your customers.

## MAKING CHOICES – WEIGHTED DECISIONS MATRICES

When faced with a multitude of choices, we can become overwhelmed with options. Too many variables, too many directions, too many chances to be wrong can be paralyzing. But there is hope. The weighted decision matrix is a tool that can help you cut through the noise, focus on what is important, and prioritize your options. Why prioritize and not just select? We'll get to that.

A decision matrix is fairly straightforward. It is simply a list of the factors that make up your decision, and a list of your options. For example, what's for dinner?

FIGURE 4.3

|  | Hot Dogs | Fish | Steak | Pasta | PB & J |
|---|---|---|---|---|---|
| Taste |  |  | X | X |  |
| Cost | X |  |  | X | X |
| Speed | X |  |  |  | X |
| Availability |  | X | X |  | X |
| Totals | 2 | 1 | 2 | 2 | 3 |

We have five options (across the top), and four criteria (down the side) upon which to judge them. Steak and pasta are judged to be the best tasting (based on a poll of the diners). Hot Dogs and Pasta are the cheapest, and so on down the list. Each "x" is worth one point. As you can see on the bottom, the highest score of 3 for PB&J indicates a choice has been made.

This is a very simple way to make a decision based on the opinions of your stakeholders. Once you have a list of options, the team decides what are the most important factors in their decision. If all else fails, you default to the standards of speed, cost and quality. You then compare the choices to each category, assign a point where appropriate, and total up the scores. Highest score wins.

*But steak doesn't taste like pasta!*

True. But the simple matrix doesn't allow for that variation. Enter the ranked decision matrix. A bit more complex, but a bit more useful, too.

FIGURE 4.4

|  | Hot Dogs | Fish | Steak | Pasta | PB & J |
|---|---|---|---|---|---|
| **Taste** | *1* | *3* | *5* | *4* | *2* |
| **Cost** | *4* | *2* | *1* | *3* | *5* |
| **Speed** | *4* | *3* | *1* | *2* | *5* |
| **Availability** | *5* | *2* | *4* | *3* | *1* |
| **Totals** | *14* | *10* | *11* | *12* | *13* |

A "ranked" decision includes a comparison of the options to each other in each category. We have five options, so we have ranked each option (5 being the highest score) for each criteria. As you can see, Hot Dogs are the new indicated dinner option. We may not like the way they taste, but they are cheap, fast and available. So our decision has changed based on those criteria.

*But I have plenty of time, and I don't want to eat food I don't like.*

Ah, another caveat. Maybe Hot Dogs shouldn't be an option at all. But if they are on the list, they must be there for a reason. So how do we indicate that the taste is more important than the speed? Our third variant is the weighted decision matrix.

FIGURE 4.5

| | Weight | Hot Dogs | | Fish | | Steak | | Pasta | | PB & J | |
|---|---|---|---|---|---|---|---|---|---|---|---|
| Taste | 5 | 1 | 5 | 3 | 15 | 5 | 25 | 4 | 20 | 2 | 10 |
| Cost | 1 | 3 | 3 | 2 | 2 | 1 | 1 | 4 | 4 | 5 | 5 |
| Speed | 1 | 4 | 4 | 2 | 2 | 1 | 1 | 3 | 3 | 5 | 5 |
| Availability | 1 | 5 | 5 | 3 | 3 | 1 | 1 | 3 | 3 | 2 | 2 |
| Totals | | | 17 | | 22 | | 28 | | 30 | | 22 |

In the "weight" column on the left, we've now indicated how important each factor is to us. Sure, we care about the cost and the time, but taste is far and away the biggest factor in our decision. We have rated is as a "5", and the scores for each option in that category will be counted five times, as opposed to once for each other category. Our new dining choice is pasta. You'll notice, though, it was not the highest ranking option in taste overall. While it may be the most important criteria, it is not the only criteria, and the scores indicate just that.

## SUMMARY

Ideas for improvement will come from multiple angles, all of which are equally valid. Top-down ideas, ideas, generated from strategic goals or leadership imperatives, will help establish credibility and impact with sponsors. Bottom-up ideas that are sourced from the HR team and the employee population, the Gemba of your organization, will provide you with ample opportunity to make changes. Those changes will alter the experience of those that perform the work and will have an ongoing positive impact. Outside in ideas, sourced through networking and social media, will provide you with insight and experience from your functional brethren in other companies.

Tools, such as the Y to X Tree, a Weighted Decision Matrix, The Kano Model, and others that we'll review in later chapters, will help you identify the right ideas to work for investing your resources. Best practices will also be of value in your continuous improvement journey, though it will be important to adapt them to your environment to maximize results.

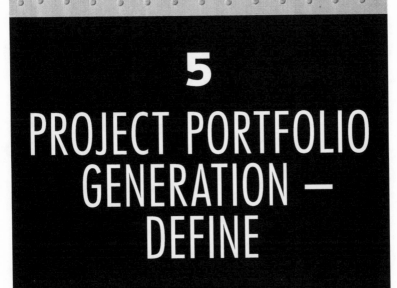

# 5
# PROJECT PORTFOLIO GENERATION — DEFINE

● ● ●

One of the most valuable tools in Six Sigma, and the one most often leveraged by other project management disciplines, is the DMAIC structure. In this chapter we will dive into this system, how it is used, and review several tools that may be of use to practitioners looking to set up their program.

DMAIC stands for Define, Measure, Analyze, Implement and Control. Those words are considered the five primary stages of a project, and you cannot move to the next step until all agree the previous has been completed. This allows for tracking progress of a project without getting too immersed in the details. Each stage has its own goals, its own requirements, and its own toolset. Understanding the system will be helpful to project management, even if it is not explicitly implemented. Here's a short overview of the stages, what they mean, and what you should be doing in each of them.

The first stage is *Define*. In short, this is where you define the issue you are trying to address and what success will look like. If you don't get this right, you'll have a hard time keeping the project on track and you may never know when you are done.

In many cases it is helpful to build a high level process map as well. At this point you aren't looking for details, but for a general understanding of who does what and where the problem (or defect) can be found.

*Measure* is all about data gathering and analysis. In my experience, this is the stage where most projects get derailed, especially in HR. Why?

Lack of information. HR can usually produce basic metrics (headcount, time to hire, budget, etc.) but often lack the more granular data that can be helpful for projects. If you want to fix a problem, you need to know everything about it. When does it happen? What else is happening at the same time? How are they related? Is this a new problem? What was it like a year ago? What is different now? Is it a new process? Is it a temporary problem? And (this is the big one) *what is the problem costing us?*

If you don't know that one, it will be tough to get the resources you may need to complete the project. Projects cost money. If they were easy and free, they wouldn't be projects. They would be done. When you are asking for resource to fix a problem, you are going to need to show someone, usually in Finance, the issue, the cost and the benefit. You want to know this as early as possible. You can't leave the Measure Stage without it. Don't even try.

The *Analyze* stage is about understanding all that data you collected in the *Measure* stage and figuring out what is really causing the problem. Here you will clearly state a theory or problem statement, evaluate the information with one or many different analysis tools, determine potential causes of the problem, collect extra data as needed, and make your best determination as to the root cause of the problem.

*Improve* is your testing stage. Once you know the root cause, you'll likely come up with lots of things that might fix the problem. Ask lots of questions, try lots of things. Test, test, test. Measure the results until you are confident that you have the answer. Be ready to show data that "proves" the defect is eliminated based on your proposed changes. Then implement those changes. You will also continue to watch data after implementation to make sure it is working as expected.

As a quick aside, one of the tenants of Six Sigma is that it isn't a real project if you already know the answer. If you know you have a leaky faucet, you don't need to run a project to reduce water usage. Fix the faucet already.

All projects end. It is one of the defining traits of a project. At some point, you won't be working on this anymore. The *Control* stage prepares you to move the project into "business as usual."

The key activities here include documenting your process and the change, training the users and stakeholders of the process, if they haven't already been part of the training, and setting up a monitor of some kind. You need to have a way of making sure the change is permanent. Personally, I've always believed that a change should make life better for the users so they won't want to go back to the old way. But that isn't always the perception, so you will want to find a way to monitor the new process, at least for a while.

As part of your project closeout, you will also want to do a postmortem to review lessons learned and recommendations for the future. While not critical to your current project, they can help set you up for long-term success.

These five stages run in a cycle. The outcome of your *Control* discussions can lead you right back to the *Define* stage of the next project. The real value of all of this is to give you a systematic, staged approach to improvement, not to make it more complex than it needs to be. Don't get hung up on the tools, the names, or the minutiae that sometimes scare people away from DMAIC. It's just a tool and an approach. Use it as a guide, but remember that the tool is only as good as the craftsman holding it.

Now that you have some understanding of the system, we will be leveraging the DMAIC process in terms of establishing your project portfolio, which could be considered a project in and of itself.

In the initial work of a project, much emphasis in the Define stage is to identify the problem or opportunity to improve. In terms of managing your project portfolio, this is the beginning of the work to identify the issues you will be attempting to resolve or the key processes you would like to improve. A critical outcome from this stage is to able to define the Y of your various process equations. The idea gathering discussed in the previous chapter is technically part of the Define stage, though it will not always be thought of that way. Once ideas are flowing, you will need to leverage other tools to organize and evaluate them.

## AFFINITY MAPPING

One of the simplest and most powerful methods of organizing several ideas is to use an affinity map. At it's simplest, this exercise moves your potential project list from any number of discrete ideas to a manageable number of idea groups, which can then be evaluated together and potentially improved or combined.

As an example, FIGURE 5.1 shows several ideas lumped together. At first glance, this is simply a loose collection of unrelated ideas that have come from multiple sources. In reality, you'll likely have far more than this to deal with at one time.

FIGURE 5.1 – UNORGANIZED IMPROVEMENT IDEAS

To begin affinity mapping, which is done by a small group, post the ideas on a wall, whiteboard or other flat surface. This is ideally done with sticky notes so you can move them around multiple times. The team then reorganizes the notes into groups. The key to this exercise is that the team members are not allowed to talk about the topics while they are reorganizing them. This may sounds difficult, but it prevents dominant team members from pushing their own ideas and keeps the exercise going until consensus is reached. Although it is not obvious at first, you will find topical trends in your notes. The team will organically identify them.

FIGURE 5.2 – IMPROVEMENT IDEAS BY TOPIC

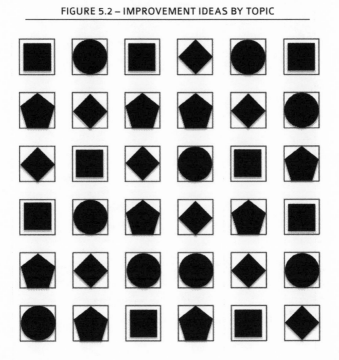

Finally, the notes should be physically reorganized into topical groups. This will happen much faster than you might imagine the first time through! In the end, you will be left with ideas that are grouped into a few general topics. These will be much easier to handled or assign to teams to review. It is often helpful to start by eliminating the duplicates and combining complementary ideas.

FIGURE 5.3 – ORGANIZED IMPROVEMENT IDEAS

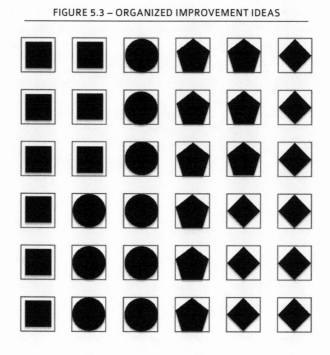

Once you have groups of ideas, you can begin making a list of the Ys in each group and evaluating those which are worthy of your improvement efforts. Recognize, however, that the ideas need not just be important to you, but also to the customer of the individual process.

## DEFINING VALUE, CTQ, AND CTP

As discussed earlier, Lean focuses on expanding the value-added activity and reducing waste. The determining factor, of course, is the opinion of the customer. Gathering this information is often referred to as Voice of Customer (VOC). It may be important to your team to pursue a major overhaul in how your training classes are advertised, but your clients may want a new way to complete their performance reviews. Even if it is a minor change, that is the area on which you will want to focus. This is a simplistic view, as changing your training programs may lead to more time and resources to work on the review process, making both far superior in the long run. But the trade-offs required by limited resources are exactly the reasons you need to make sure you understand your options before you invest your time.

Value is defined in VOC in many ways—the most common are Quality (adherence to specifications, services, features, and reliability); Cost (initial price, repair costs, residual value, amount and type of capital required); and Speed (cycle, delivery, setup and response time). FIGURE 5.4 is an old saying and has become one of the most told myths in business. The truth is you needn't choose between these three key components, as they are all complementary in a Lean system. Reducing waste improves your quality, reduces your cost, and increases your speed. The idea that you must choose between the two is outdated and, frankly, limiting thinking.

FIGURE 5.4 – THE CLASSIC BUSINESS MYTH

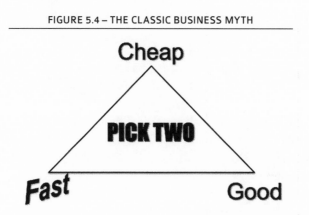

When looking at these three factors and determining what is important in your process to your customer, we consider two components: Critical to Quality (CTQ) and Critical to Process (CTP). CTQ are parameters set forth by your customer that must be met, usually in the form of a defined metric. That metric is there to support a level of service by defining a key activity. This is commonly documented in a Service Level Agreement (SLA). (In terms of the process equation, the SLA is the X, while the service is the Y. As anyone who deals with SLAs can tell you, there are always more Xs in play than can be defined!)

Suppose you are responsible for the management of an HR shared-service team, and your primary goal is to keep employee satisfaction with your service at a high level (seventy-five percent or better) while managing costs and promoting certain benefits, such as tuition reimbursement. Your VOC research, discovered through surveys, feedback sessions, and focus groups, has indicated that employees care most about the team being responsive first and foremost. The ability to provide a concise and accurate answer finished as a close second.

The SLA you draft in response could outline easily measured and reported metrics, as it always should, around these VOC issues. Setting a goal of responding to ninety-five percent of all employee inquiries within twenty-four hours, in conjunction with a goal of fifty percent first-call resolutions, would address these issues. Your SLAs, because they are focused on the needs of the customer, would be considered CTQ metrics.

At the same time, reviewing these goals with your team may help you uncover key aspects of your internal processes that must be addressed or improved in order to meet these goals. For example, the HR team must receive the inquiries in a timely manner in order to fashion a response, so the uptime on your email and phone systems are critical. A target of ninety-nine percent uptime in these areas is not uncommon. The team may also decide that they need quick access to critical information in order to meet the SLA for first call resolution, such as a robust case and knowledge management software platform. The establishment of such could then be established as a goal to be completed by a specified time. These two items would be Critical to Process (CTP), in that failing to meet them will prevent the team from working effectively.

While CTP issues can be identified through many of the bottom-up idea generation methods discussed earlier in this book, there are several methods available for determining your CTQ objectives. For example, you may seek out customer-specific aspects through feedback systems or customer interviews. You might hear from your HR team or business partners about their needs and the feedback they have received. You might also keep an eye on industry trends and competitor offerings, just to be sure you are staying at the desired level of service as compared to the market overall. These are all very valid sources of information and could be used to augment your idea generation work.

## SIPOC

Once the CTQ and CTP parameters are established, you should be prepared to look at the overall process a bit more. This will not include in-depth process design, as you will still be making decisions around which project ideas to commission. You will, however, need to have a high level of understanding of the process in question, which is where a SIPOC becomes useful.

SIPOC stands for Suppliers, Inputs, Process, Outputs and Customers. It is intended to give you a general understanding of who is involved, how they contribute, and the work that goes into a process. FIGURE 5.5 offers an example of a completed SIPOC for the process of answering an employee inquiry.

### FIGURE 5.5 – A COMPLETED SIPOC

| Suppliers | Inputs | Process | Outputs | Customers |
|---|---|---|---|---|
| Employee | Inquiry | Employee calls | Answer | HR |
| Vendor | Software | HR answers | Record of call | Management |
| Telecom | Phone System | Inquiry stated | | Employee |
| | | HR queries KB | | |
| | | Answer given | | |
| | | Call ends | | |

In this example, we assume the inquiry will come through a phone call and will be answered by the HR representative. They will receive the call, listen to the question or issue, search the knowledge base for information, respond to the employee, and disconnect the call. While this particular SIPOC assumes a discussion via phone, the process would not be notably different for an email, chat, or face-to-face inquiry. The suppliers in this example are the employees (supplying the inquiry); the vendor who has supplied the software used by HR, as well as the email system and phone software (which could, of course, be multiple vendors); and the telecommunications provider (which could be easily changed to an Internet provider). The inputs in this case are the inquiry itself, the knowledge base, and the telecommunication equipment. The process is as outlined above, with our outputs listed as the information that was requested and, in all likelihood, a record of the call for metrics purposes. Our customers are defined as the employee, management (who will receive the metrics for review), and the HR team, who are users of the systems in place for the process. All of these customers will need to be considered when work to revise the process is discussed!

## STAKEHOLDER IDENTIFICATION

As you begin to consider the customers of each process, you may start to realize there is a long list of interest parties for each part of your business. The mindset of these stakeholders, as they are known, will also have a significant impact on your ability to make changes.

Before spending much time on the whims of each group, it is important to note that not everyone who cares about a process is considered a stakeholder. In fact, there are only two factors that go into deciding if one should be considered a true stakeholder:

1) **They have money.**

2) **They have power.**

Meeting either (or both) of these prerequisites means the party in question can either provide or withhold resources, including money, time, support, or political support, to your project. If they can offer neither of these, then they are not truly stakeholders (although they may still be a customer and therefore important overall).

Once you have identified your stakeholders, at least at the preliminary level, you will need to determine how they are likely to feel about a change in the process. Based on your best information, a Stakeholder Exercise and Stakeholder Analysis will give you a quick summary of their current position. It will also give you an idea of the level of support you will need from them and what steps you should take to make that change.

The Stakeholder Exercise simply lists each party, their level of influence over the project, and the resources they may provide or withhold. In FIGURE 5.6, you can see a simple example of the stakeholders for a project to revise how HR handles an incoming employee call.

FIGURE 5.6 – A COMPLETED STAKEHOLDER EXERCISE

| Stakeholder | Influence | Involvement |
|---|---|---|
| Chris Grey, VP of HR | Resources, Funding | Project Champion |
| Jamie Brown, VP of IT | May resist system changes | Owns IT systems |
| Pat White, Dir of HRSS | Approval over any process change | Process Owner |
| Alex Black, Dir of Telcom | Oversees system contracts | Vendor Management |

A Stakeholder Analysis is a bit more in depth, and can often be left until the project itself has been accepted and is underway. Because project success is so dependent on the amount of work put into stakeholder buy-in, having this information up front may prevent you from selecting a project that has no real chance of success. FIGURE 5.7 provides a look at a completed Stakeholder Analysis for the same project.

FIGURE 5.7 – A COMPLETED STAKEHOLDER ANALYSIS

| Key Stakeholder | Strongly Against | Moderately Against | Neutral | Moderately Supportive | Strongly Supportive | Reasons for current position. |
|---|---|---|---|---|---|---|
| Chris Grey VP of HR | | | | X | | Team performance |
| Jamie Brown VP of IT | | | X → | | | Budget not planned for changes |
| Pat White Dir of HRSS | | | | X → | | Must approve any change |
| Alex Black Dir of Telcom | | X → | | | | Strong relationship with current vendor |

As you can see, the biggest hurdle identified at this stage is in the potential need to change vendors and the resistance the project would likely face from Alex Black. For that reason, it may be prudent to have an initial conversation regarding the project before moving forward.

## SUMMARY

Investing the time early in the project selection phase to understand the scope of each process will make a tremendous difference in your success rate later. Understanding the process value from the customer's perspective, including the CTQ and CTP elements, will allow you a better view of what needs to be accomplished and what the improvement target should be. Finally, taking the time up front to identify the project stakeholders, especially those who may be opposed to changes, will allow you to avoid choosing a project that is doomed to failure.

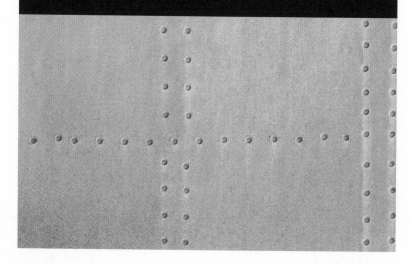

# 6
# PROJECT PORTFOLIO GENERATION – MEASURE

● ● ●

In the Measure stage, we start looking at our project Ys and ensuring we can measure their current state. Some Ys will be very nebulous, and therefore difficult to identify. It is best to know this information now, rather than after resources have been committed to the project.

To the chagrin of some, this means taking the time to review some statistical measures that you will find helpful. This is not intended to be a comprehensive review of in-depth analytical tools. Instead, this will be a review of the very least you need to understand in order to evaluate data and compare data sets for meaningful changes. Without this knowledge, it will be difficult to ever prove you've made a difference through your work.

## RANGE, MEAN, MEDIAN, MODE

Any set of numbers, when all taken together, are known as a range. When you are collecting information for process performance during any set amount of time, be it a week, month, year or more, you are collecting a range of data for that time. The R for each data set is defined by the largest number less the smallest number, as shown in FIGURE 6.1.

FIGURE 6.1 – THE RANGE OF A SET OF DATA

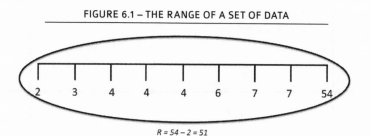

$$R = 54 - 2 = 51$$

When people speak of an "average" value, the savvy statistician knows there are three possible meanings. While marketers have used them to knead and prod data for years, they are still not terms that are commonly used in business.

Mean refers to the central value on a line representing all values, as seen in FIGURE 6.2. This is what most people are using for "average." The problem with mean is that it can be easily skewed by outliers, or values that are far removed from the center. In this example, one value on the far right (fifty-four) moves the mean all the way to ten, when all other values in the range are below that.

### FIGURE 6.2 – THE MEAN VALUE OF THIS RANGE

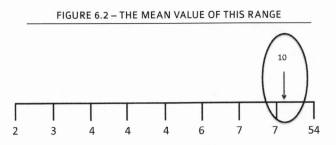

Median is the central point of the range, with an equal number or responses on each side. While this may seem like the same as mean at first, FIGURE 6.3 shows that the median and the mean are quite different in this example. In a great number of analyses, you will find both the mean and the median included. They give, not only an idea of the "average" value, but also help to detect any outliers just by nature of the difference between the two.

Finally, mode refers to the most common data point in the range, as seen in FIGURE 6.3. This could be anywhere in the data set, including the first or last value. Mode is a general indicator of where in the range you are likely to see larger groups of responses, though by itself is somewhat limited in usefulness.

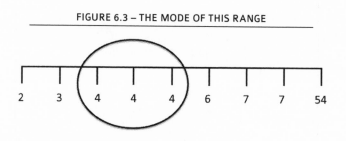

FIGURE 6.3 – THE MODE OF THIS RANGE

2    3    4    4    4    6    7    7    54

## GRAPH TYPES AND USAGE

With the plethora of types available and the ease of producing them, thanks to Excel and other spreadsheet tools, it is no wonder that we are constantly bombarded with graphs of all sorts in the workplace. Sadly, too few people understand the correct graph type to use for their data, and too many people understand how to use graphs to hide information from the reader. For those reasons, let's review the basic graph types you are likely to use or read and how each of them can be used to emphasize or hide important information.

The most common types of graphs you will either see or use are pie charts, bar charts, line charts, and histograms.

## PIE CHARTS

Used to examine distribution of resources as compared to a whole, the pie chart is the most common used for examining survey results or workload distribution. For this reason, they are very common in both mass media and in workforce metrics. Pie charts are the most trustworthy in the set, as they are used to display relationships against the whole. Other than mislabeling data or combining groups, it is very difficult to hide key data elements in this type of graph.

FIGURE 6.4 – PIE CHART: DISTRIBUTION OF PATTERNS

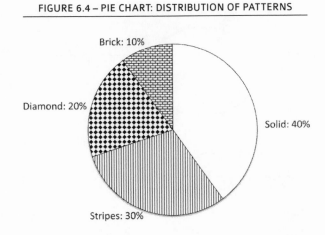

## BAR CHARTS

These are also used for comparisons but are for comparing data sets against each other instead of against the whole. For that reason, bar charts can be much more difficult to read accurately. For example, the FIGURE 6.5 and 6.6 show exactly the same information—sales volume for a three different locations. Notice that FIGURE 6.5 shows a near unchanged output over that time, while FIGURE 6.6 give the impression of a significant leap in performance!

FIGURE 6.5 – BAR CHART: SALES REPORT BY OFFICE

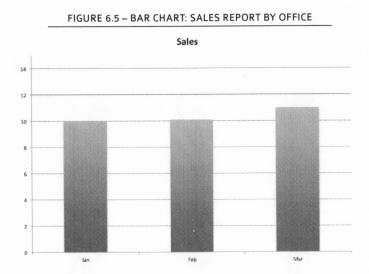

FIGURE 6.6 – BAR CHART: SALES REPORT BY OFFICE

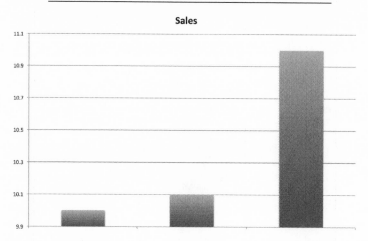

**Sales**

The difference in the two is the scale of the axis on the left. Notice the difference in the beginning and the end points, and you will see why the second looks dramatically different. By a simple adjustment in the display choices, you can tell two very different stories.

## LINE CHARTS

The most appropriate use of a line chart is to measure a trend over time. While you may see this function graphed in bar chart form, be aware that line charts are the correct format for this data. Line charts are also very useful in comparing trends between two different populations, as shown in FIGURE 6.7.

One of the dangers of this type of graph is having two data sets that are unrelated displayed together, as if there is a comparison that should be drawn between the two. FIGURE 6.7 appears to be a comparison of sales trends for two locations, with one clearly outperforming the other. However, the data for one set is in dollars, while the other is in units. This is less about obfuscating information and more about poor use of the tool, but it is still misleading to the casual observer.

## FIGURE 6.7 – LINE CHART: SALES COMPARISON BY BRANCH

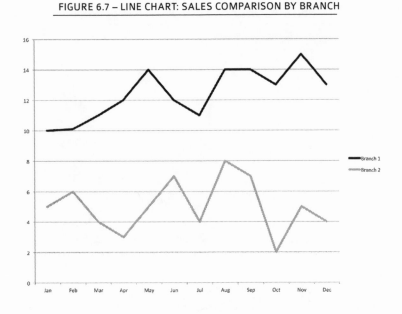

A second common danger of this type of line chart is drawing the conclusion of a causal relationship between two sets of data when it may only be, in fact, a strong correlation. The difference is that in a causal relationship, changes in the first data set are the reason there are changes in the second set. In a correlated set, one data set tends to move the same as the second but does not have any influence over that data. For example, there is a clear causal relationship between average daytime temperature and the consumption of ice cream per person. This is an elementary example, to be sure, but one that does not require a great deal of thought.

## FIGURE 6.8 – LINE CHART: ICE CREAM AND DROWNING TRENDS

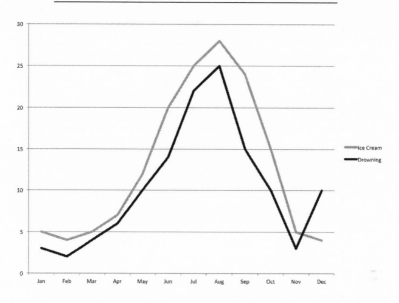

In the same way, there is a clear relationship between drowning deaths and ice cream consumption, as they tend to rise and fall at the same time and general rate, as shown in FIGURE 6.8. Does this mean people are drowning in ice cream? Of course not. As with most correlations, there is another factor at work. In this case it is the average temperature, which drives people to eat ice cream and go swimming. Higher water activity naturally leads to a high rate of water fatality. Graphing both data sets may lead to a false assumption of causality, so it is important to understand what information lies behind the chart.

## HISTOGRAMS

Finally, the histogram is a method of plotting results from a single process. While technically a type of bar chart, it is used to show the occurrences of a particular score or result. The data displayed is often referred to as a "population," which means the information is all of the same data type. The power of the histogram is that it can quickly show that there may indeed be more than one population, which means a new X was introduced at some point in the process and more than one Y is being tracked. FIGURE 6.9 is an example of a "normal distribution" of test scores, sometimes known as a bell-shaped curve.

FIGURE 6.9 – HISTOGRAM: TEST SCORES

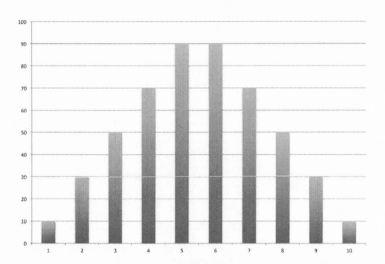

FIGURE 6.10 shows a similar data set, only this includes the scores from two classes. As you may deduce, the presence of two peaks implies there is a second population on this chart.

Histograms are useful in examining data sets to ensure you have controlled possible variables in your data and have narrowed the Xs down to those you can control. They will also be useful as we reach the analyze stage, as they are combined with line charts to create a new tool.

FIGURE 6.10 – HISTOGRAM: TEST SCORES

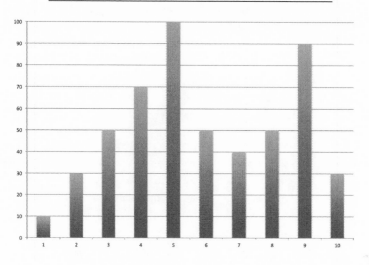

## IDENTIFYING GOOD METRICS

I worked on a project to create standard processes for the global HR practice with an organization for more than two years. One of the questions that came up repeatedly was around measurement. How do you measure adoption rate of the processes? How do you know when people aren't using them? And what are you going to do about it if someone doesn't want to use them?

We developed a self-assessment to see if a location was aware of the processes and if they were using them, as well as gather their feedback. But we were after more than compliance. We were after the usefulness of the processes and improvement opportunities. We could record adoption rates from there, if we really want to, but it was all based on self-reporting, which everyone knows can be spotty at best.

More to the point, though, the question is why would we care? We should only want to invest the time and effort into measuring and reporting something if it was important. Is it important to know if our process are being used? After years of working on the project, I'm convinced the answer is no.

Standard processes are, in most cases, a building block toward something else. In this case, they were pre-work for an HRMS and self-service implementation. We built upon the basic framework with regional/country adaptations that outlined the changes needed for local laws, and then built out the technology and tools on top of that. The use of the standard processes was, to me, secondary. If it were the end goal, it would certainly warrant reporting. But as an intermediate step, I'm not so sure.

As I've said before, new processes/tools/widgets are only going to be successful if they are better than the old version (or at least are perceived by the user to be better). If our long term deliverables, including those systems and tools, weren't better than the manual way of doing work, we would have failed, and no one would use them. If we did present a new system that was an improvement, people would flock to it. And then the measurement of that interim point isn't valuable.

Trying to measure the success of an intermediate step is, I think, a distraction. Feedback is good, of course, but should be gathered in the context of preparing for the next step. More importantly, trying to measure usage of a manual process would be far more resource intensive than it is worth. And once you know that, why would you spend any more time working on it?

If you are building a solution to meet the needs of the user, it is their feedback (or lack thereof) that should matter. So keep your communication lines open, listen to them, and give them what they need.

As an example, I once had a package sent to me via USPS Express Mail with Delivery Confirmation. I expected the package to arrive on Wednesday. I watched with excitement as the package was shipped early, and was a bit surprised when I saw the delivery confirmation for Saturday. I checked the mail...no package. I checked the porch...no package. The garage was equally bereft of packagy goodness. No one had seen, heard, touched or sensed a package. Not good.

I contacted the USPS online to express my concern. They assigned a case number and let me know they would be in touch within two days. Three days passed with no word. I followed up diligently and politely, but no response came. Finally, I dropped into my local USPS office and questioned them. They had indeed heard of the issue, they said, and were looking into it. They spoke with the carrier, who let them know she had taken the package up our driveway and left it on the porch. Still not good.

While this was going on, I had another package confirmed as delivered. It was also nowhere to be seen. Lack of good now twice confirmed.

Days later, I received a call that my packages were never delivered, and were waiting at the USPS office to be picked up.

My concern was not that my packages were late. They weren't terribly valuable, important or hard to replace. My bigger concern was over the "confirmed delivery" feature, which apparently is just an indicator that someone scanned the package and marked it confirmed. No indicator of where it was confirmed, despite the easy access to GPS systems these days for geocaching as a service. (UPS or FedEx, that's a free idea. Take it. Never lose a delivery again!)

This kind of experience makes me look at metrics and think, "How easy would it be to get around this?" Good metrics are indicative of trends. Point measures are much easier to manipulate, but measuring performance over time helps to smooth outliers and eliminate the potential impact of one biased observer. Discrete measures can be manipulated short term. Need to reduce headcount? Hold a RIF, hire them back as temps! Need to reduce your expenses for this quarter? Hold that expense report until the end of the month! Trying to influence HR Return on Investment? Or HR to headcount ratios? Or days per hire over the last year? Much more difficult.

That's why those metrics are more meaningful. They are truer measures of performance and harder to manipulate. Take a look at your metrics and think about how to make them look better. If you can find a way to change the number without a change in behavior, that metric is bad.

When we fail to deliver, who pays the most? Airline flight delays cost passengers more than inconvenience — $16.7 billion more — according to a study delivered to the Federal Aviation Administration a few years ago.

The FAA-funded study looks at the cost to passengers for flight delays in 2007, the latest year for which complete data was available when researchers began working on the study.

Unlike past studies of the impact of flight delays, researchers looked more broadly at the costs associated with flight delays, including passengers' lost time waiting for flights and then scrambling to make other arrangements when flights are canceled.

The cost to airlines for delays was $8.3 billion, mostly for crew, fuel and maintenance. Overall, the cost was $33 billion, including to other parts of the economy. But one finding of the study is that more than half the cost associated with flight delays is borne by passengers.

Over half of the cost passed directly to the customers. These are people who have already paid a good deal of money for their ticket, not to mention their bag. Extra fees are invented seemingly daily to boost the revenue of the airlines, and now we see the passengers are the ones who really suffer from poor performance.

It's no surprise, of course, and it happens in your business, too. When HR creates a bad process, or rolls out a broken tool, or tries to enforce an ill-conceived policy, who pays for it? Usually the other departments, mangers, employees and leaders. HR loses some creditability, but the cost is borne elsewhere. This is why it is so important for young HR professionals to spend time outside of HR, experience the impact of those bad decisions, the vague policies, and the misleading or misaligned metrics. Have it done to you, not with you, and see what happens.

Metrics are critical to running your HR practice, but far too many HR practitioners haven't been taught what they really need to know about them. Here's a few tips that might be helpful.

- **No one really cares about headcount.** How can you tell? Ask a simple question. If the headcount next week is ten fewer than last week, what will you do about it? The answer is usually "it depends." And that's the right one. Headcount is an indicator, an important denominator for some metrics that are truly indicative of what is happening. But alone, it's almost meaningless.

- **No one really cares about straight turnover.** What they care about is the cause of turnover, and what can be done about it. To deal with it, you have to understand what kind of turnover you are dealing with (Voluntary? Involuntary? Regrettable? Retirees? Internal movement?), and then you can start to find the root cause.

- **Business leaders watch trends more than numbers.** Don't get hung up in the minutia of reporting. Look for trends that are playing out over weeks, or even better months, instead of day to day. Businesses are run that way. Your practice should be too.

- **But know the numbers, too.** Nothing will sap your credibility faster than presenting a set of trends and not being able to talk about the details. Present the important part and tell the story that needs to be told. But be ready when they ask for more, and be able to discuss not only the details, but what they mean to the business. That will bring your credibility up, and help you guide your partners in making better decisions for your population.

- **Finally, learn to distinguish between correlation and causation.** Sure there are more drownings when ice cream sales are at their peak. But few people drown in ice cream, right? Knowing the difference can help you guide a business leader to hire lifeguards, not bad butter pecan.

## SUMMARY

The ability to accurately measure and communicate values for the Y of your process is critical to your success. Simple statistical concepts such as range, mean, median, and mode are all important in terms of understanding the information you see. In addition, there are several types of graphical data representations that should be leveraged depending on the type of information being displayed. Understanding the difference between bar charts, line charts, pie charts and histograms can not only help you tell the story behind your information, but can keep you from being misled by data others are sharing.

# 7
# PROJECT PORTFOLIO GENERATION – ANALYZE

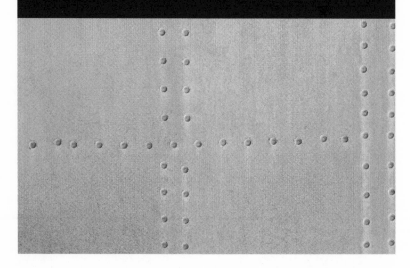

● ● ●

Once you have determined you can measure your Y, it is time to start finding the Xs that will be the target of improvement. In the Analyze phase, we dive into the process and look for specific areas that may be influential in adjusting the Y. Understanding which of your potential improvement areas will return the greatest result will be a major influence in how your resources are deployed.

## FISHBONE DIAGRAMS

Once you have an idea of the issues you will pursue, it is time to start thinking about the root cause of failure or suboptimal performance in that area. This continues along the path of discovering as much as possible about a potential project before committing resources and will help you be more precise in the work to be done by the eventual project team. Known by several names, including cause-and-effect diagrams and Ishikawa diagrams (after Kaoru Ishikawa, their creator), fishbone diagrams provide a structured approach to brainstorming potential failure points in a process. To begin a diagram, as seen in FIGURE 7.1, is sketched out that includes six branches, each to represent a different area of investigation: people, materials, processes, environment, equipment, and management.

FIGURE 7.1 – SAMPLE FISHBONE DIAGRAM

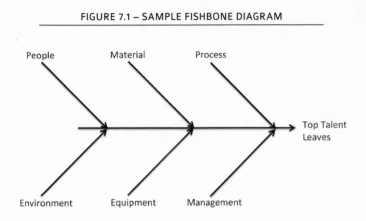

Then, ideally with a team, examine each of the six areas for potential issues, improvements, or causes of failure. People will include anyone involved in the process, including suppliers, customers, and maybe individuals or groups. Materials involve everything from the raw materials that begin the process to the final product provided to a customer. Processes (sometimes referred to as methods) include how the work is done, any documentation that is provided, and any laws or policies that influence the work. The environment entails the conditions under which the work is done, be it physical, mental, political, or other. Equipment includes any tools needed to complete the work or that are involved in transforming the materials. Finally, management involves not only the way in which the process is overseen, but also the metrics that are used to guide performance and quality. In FIGURE 7.2, you will see a fishbone diagram that documents reasons top talent leaves an organization. It is not unusual to encounter potential causes that may fit into more than one category. Capturing the idea is most important, not where it is listed on the diagram. Your goal is to identify the potential areas of concern for further examination, not to make a final classification of each item.

FIGURE 7.2 – COMPLETED FISHBONE DIAGRAM

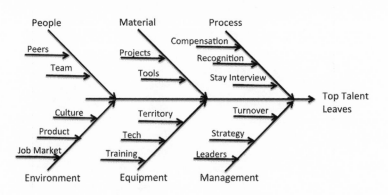

## FIVE WHYS

If you are still having trouble finding the issues within your process, there is another simple yet effective tool that is used by children all around the world. It goes something like this:

"WHYWHYWHYWHYWHY?????"

Small children ask "Why?" approximately 18,000 times per day. Like many Lean tools, Sakichi Toyoda, one of the driving forces behind Toyota's achievements, used it heavily at first. This method, generally known as "five whys," is a simple way to get to the root cause of a problem. I think we can all agree that the first answer will likely get you another question, if you care enough to keep asking. For instance:

"Why do we have a difficult time finding qualified engineering applicants when unemployment is so high?"

"We aren't reaching the right candidates and instead spend time combing through stacks of resumes that don't include the skills we need."

OK, fair enough. But that's not the root cause of the issue, right? It's just another layer down. So we keep going....

"Why aren't we reaching the right candidates?"

"The job we are trying to fill has a very specific skillset, which is hard to find either internally or externally."

Hmm. Interesting.

"Why can't we find the skills internally?"

"We don't have a training program designed around the job. While it's an important role, we haven't worked to grow our own talent in this area."

After just three questions, we are in a much different place than where we started. Now we are discussing our core beliefs around talent management instead of a recruiting and marketing problem. That's what root cause analysis is all about. You go where the questions and answers lead you. And until you get to the root of a problem, you'll never really fix anything.

Why five? Because. That's why. Will five always get you the root cause? Nope. Sometimes three will do, sometimes ten. But you have to start somewhere.

There are a few drawbacks to this tool. First, you can't come up with root causes you don't know about, so you are limited to the knowledge of the person answering you. You shouldn't ever rely on one person to answer the question, so you will need to seek out multiple perspectives. Also, you're likely to get a different set of answers from each person you talk to. This will provide you with a greater number of potential improvement ideas. Most major issues have several contributing factors, so your task is to determine which are the most significant. Getting input from several stakeholders can help you scope the issue appropriately and keep you aware of the related issues that may come up later.

There are no templates for this tool, so it can be deployed at any time and place. Just about any work you are doing, be it a case study, fishbone diagram, benefits design, or group therapy, can benefit from dropping in the occasional set of whys. You may be surprised to where the questions lead you.

## PARETO DIAGRAM

In the year 1906, an Italian economist and engineer named Vilfredo Pareto noticed in his studies that eighty percent of the land in Italy was owned by twenty percent of the population. He observed similar ratios in his garden, his work, and aspects of society. So was born the Pareto Principle, which essentially states that eighty percent of your results (or your Y, in our process equation) are driven by twenty percent of your inputs (or Xs). In truth, Pareto did not state that 80/20 were magic numbers, and in fact observed that the percentage could be anywhere from fifty percent to one hundred percent, depending on the size of the population. But the 80/20 rule has been a fair estimate in many cases and is the most common version known today.

From this we can extrapolate that while we may not see a distribution exactly to that ratio, we can be sure that not all Xs are created equal. Because we have a limited number of resources with which to execute projects, we must examine our Xs to decide which ones to focus on. To get a visual representation of the distribution, we create a Pareto chart by combining a line chart and a histogram, as shown in FIGURE 7.3.

FIGURE 7.3 - PARETO DIAGRAM – ENERGY CONSUMPTION

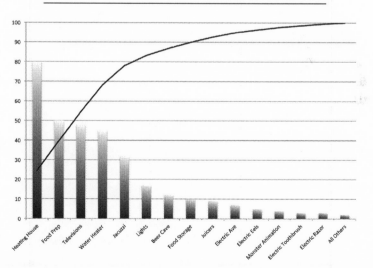

The line chart added to the histogram shows the cumulative percentage of the total represented at each point of the histogram. Clearly the steeply increasing line begins to level off a few columns in. While you could calculate the point at which eighty percent is reached, it doesn't require even that small amount of mathematics to realize there isn't much value in the data points to the far right. As the items on the chart will represent the Xs in this process equation, you will clearly be best served pursuing the inputs on the left.

As you examine your project options, creating a Pareto diagram of the cost or potential payback of your choices will likely create a similar result. You will quickly realize that not all Xs are created equal.

## LIVING PARETO DIAGRAMS

When you are living in a Lean world, part of your job is looking at certain metrics every day. When one of your metrics goes off the rails, it becomes the leader's job to determine what is causing the defect and then define the corrective action. The living Pareto Diagram, a variant of the original, will help you do that in real time. Let's take a closer look at FIGURE 7.4.

FIGURE 7.4

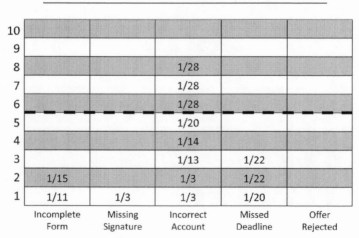

| | Incomplete Form | Missing Signature | Incorrect Account | Missed Deadline | Offer Rejected |
|---|---|---|---|---|---|
| 10 | | | | | |
| 9 | | | | | |
| 8 | | | 1/28 | | |
| 7 | | | 1/28 | | |
| 6 | | | 1/28 | | |
| 5 | | | 1/20 | | |
| 4 | | | 1/14 | | |
| 3 | | | 1/13 | 1/22 | |
| 2 | 1/15 | | 1/3 | 1/22 | |
| 1 | 1/11 | 1/3 | 1/3 | 1/20 | |

In this example, the number of times a defect occurs is on the left side, while reasons for defect are on the bottom. The dates in the grid are a list of each time that particular incident occurred. Posted in an area with easy access, this tool allows you to capture data at the point of failure each time. But even more important is the dashed horizontal line crossing the chart. That line is the upper control limit, or the indicator that a defect occurs enough to notice. If the number of incidents crosses that line, it's time to take action.

From there you have your choice of tools, of course. Five Whys, fishbone diagram, or whatever fits the situation. But this tool allows you track how often you have a defect, what caused it, and when it is time to act.

## MEASURING YOUR IMPACT

It will also be important at this stage to define how you will measure your success for projects that are implemented. You will likely need a few standard metrics to report out to leadership, and they can provide great insight into your effectiveness.

The first step is to estimate the expected savings from executing the project. Savings are classified in three general categories: hard savings, soft savings, and cost avoidance.

Hard savings, also known as "the only savings that matter," result in an overall reduction in your budgeted expenditures. This includes any budget in the organization, not just the HR team. You may find your projects impact budgets other than yours in many cases. While some Lean plans place emphasize savings within each functional budget area, many consider this a limiting view that leads to internal conflict over savings gained by working together. At this stage, you should be less concerned about who will see the savings and focus instead on the potential overall impact.

While nice to have, soft savings rarely appear on the balance sheet. A common soft savings is time spent working on a task. In theory, reducing the number of hours required by a process from ten to five each week results in a savings of 250 hours per year. Multiplied by the wage of the person responsible to perform the work will provide a nice dollar amount, but unless that person is removed from the organization or their hours reduced, your cost will remain neutral. Soft savings are still valuable, though, and should be reported alongside hard savings as an indicator that you have improved working conditions and eliminated waste beyond the initial savings estimate.

Cost avoidance is a measure of what would have been potentially spent on a problem but was instead prevented by the project execution. For example, implementing a case management software package will significantly reduce the cost of discovery in the event of a discrimination charge, but those dollars are not in the "planned" expenditures under normal business conditions. Projects in the area are sometimes still approved as a worthy use of resources or are needed to meet compliance requirements, but they are always tracked separately from a savings standpoint.

Once you have estimated the savings for a project, you will need to determine if it is worth pursuing, and that will usually mean meeting a threshold for expenditures determined at the highest level of the organization. The most common of these is ROI. A classic financial measure, this target is based on the concept that you can expect a certain level of return, if given the opportunity to invest capital in any number of ways. This target may fluctuate based on the economic environment, the debt level of the company, or any other number of factors. What will be important for you to know is what your particular organization's threshold will be for your fiscal environment. It should be no surprise that running a project will likely require some level of capital investment, such as salaries of the team, new software, changes in machinery, or other expenditure. Project ROI determines if that use of resources will bring a greater return than other avenues of investment.

The formula for ROI is often expressed as a percentage, and is calculated by dividing your net gain (savings less project cost) by your project cost. For example, if your project will save an estimated $100,000, but your cost is estimated to also be $100,000, you will have a zero percent ROI and are not likely to receive project funding. Performing the same work with only $10,000 invested will result in a project ROI of nine hundred percent, a fine return on capital. Most projects will be far lower than this, though you may find some high ROI opportunities as you start your program. The low-hanging fruit will be important to gain quick credibility with your leadership team, and you should focus at least half of your time in the first year on these types of opportunities.

Another common measure of project value is the payback period. This measure compares the project cost and savings to determine how long it will take for the project to pay for itself and is normally expressed in years. For example, a project that saves $100,000 annually and costs $50,000 will have a two-year payback period. This measure emphasizes projects that return ongoing savings, as opposed to a one-time impact, and can be used to evaluate the speed of the savings. And the ROI is the same regardless of the time required. (Your organization will likely impose a time limit for savings to be included in an ROI calculation, though there is not a prescribed length of time in general.)

## YOUR BEST RESOURCE

Many HR practitioners have struggled with project valuation and have found when a project is completed they were far off the mark. This often happens for many reasons, not the least of which are a lack of familiarity with the tools and the tendency to overestimate the impact of pet projects. Therefore, you should always work with a partner to evaluate projects. This could be done in your project selection session, which we will discuss in the next chapter, but ideally it will be done prior to selection. Having your projects reviewed by a member of the finance team or a business analyst could be significantly helpful in ensuring you understand the true impact of a potential change. That will, in turn, help you select the best way to deploy your resources.

## SUMMARY

Measuring the potential impact of your project starts with understanding what the Xs are, as well as realizing that not all of the inputs are worth pursuing. By examining the total set and determining which Xs really drive value, you will be able to start understanding the value and cost of each project. Fishbone diagrams and Five Whys exercises will help you seek out the issues, their causes, and the potential impact of making a change. Then through ROI, payback period, or some other measure defined in your organization, you will be able to compare the projects to each other and select those that provide the best chance to improve your practice in a way that is meaningful to the organization's bottom line.

**8**
# PROJECT PORTFOLIO GENERATION – IMPLEMENT

● ● ●

Having a thorough understanding of your project options is the foundation of strong project portfolio. In the implementation stage, it is time to choose the commissioned projects, select project champions and leaders, and create the project charter to start the improvement work.

## DEPLOYMENT SESSIONS

Committing to a set of projects requires that leadership agrees on how resources will be spent. The level of leadership and necessary agreement will vary based on how ambitious your plans are, but because you will need resources for running projects of any significance, your leaders will need to be engaged.

The best place to start is to gather the ideas you have cultivated already, as well as asking the rest of the team to do the same. This should provide you with a robust slate of potential projects or at least a list of issues to address. Each member of the team should present his or her list, explaining as follows: the issue and opportunity as he or she sees it, expectations for savings/ROI/payback period, and any supporting documentation that may be relevant. This allows the team to discuss and ensure they have an appropriate level of understanding of each opportunity before making decisions. Then compile these ideas into a master list, combining duplicate or similar issues. This would be a fine place to bring back the affinity mapping exercise to help classify your ideas quickly. The next task is to evaluate these ideas against each other so you can make a final selection.

## CALCULATING ROI

One of the most difficult things to do is determine what a project might be worth at this stage. Because we will need an estimate for our next step, it is important to have some idea of project value before moving on. In lieu of hard data, there are a few simple assumptions that, if agreed upon, can be used to get past the wailing and gnashing of teeth of ROI and get to work on improvements.

*People are worth more to the organization than they are paid.* Tough to admit, but its a natural rule of business. Companies should have revenues exceeding their costs, and should far exceed their payroll. Simple. You can extrapolate that to determine how much a position is paid per day will be less than it is worth per day, and calculate cost of time to fill from there. Not accurate, but representative. And low.

*When you can't verify the accuracy of a number, we can often verify the validity of a trend.* That's good enough in some cases. Again, weight the cost of getting accuracy against the value of knowing the "real" number. Headcount comes to mind. It's not the absolute number that matters, it is the trend over time that you have to watch. If you aren't likely to take a specific action when the number shifts month to month, then you want trends, not discrete data points.

*Flat line cost changes are, in most cases, not sustainable.* You can't set a target of reducing costs 10% each year and expect to eventually reach a zero cost process in most cases. You need to have something with which to compare your costs, like headcount, revenue or production. You can't always reduce flat line costs, but you can always work to reduce relative costs.

It's not everything you will need, but it's a place to start.

## EFFORT/IMPACT MATRIX

This tool is a fine choice for making decisions about your project opportunities. Having identified the expected financial impact already, you will need only to decide what the criteria for evaluation will be. Then, as a team, agree on each project's value. An effort/impact matrix will then help you make decisions as a group by presenting projects in an objective way.

Criteria and values will vary by organization and may even change between departments. FIGURE 8.1 is a suggested set of categories and values for the project impact.

FIGURE 8.1 – PROJECT IMPACT MATRIX VALUE

| Category | Description | Low | Medium | High |
|---|---|---|---|---|
| Hard Savings | Expected dollars saved through the project | Under $10k | $10k to $100k | $100k or more |
| Number of Task Owners | No. of employees involved in the work being changed | Under 10 | 10 – 25 | 25 or more |
| Scope | Geographic area of impact | Local | Regional | Global |
| Strategic Connection | Levels of X removed from any strategic Y | 3 or more | 2 | 1 |

Next, review the project effort. FIGURE 8.2 is a set of examples that may be used or modified as needed. Once the cutoffs have been established, each project can then be measured against them, and you can reach a consensus as to its category score. Because there will sometimes be disagreement or uncertainty in these numbers, it is best to take a conservative approach in each area.

FIGURE 8.2 – PROJECT EFFORT MATRIX VALUE

| Category | Description | Low | Medium | High |
|---|---|---|---|---|
| Project Expense | Cost to assemble and run the project team | Less than $1K | $1K to $5K | $5K or more |
| Time to Complete | Time expected to realize first project savings | <1 month | 1 - 3 months | >3 months |
| Functions Impacted | Number of functional groups involved in process | 1 | 2 - 3 | >3 |
| IT System Impact | Likely changes to existing It structure or contracts | None | Data or Structure | New purchase |

Once the team has reached agreement on the scores for each project, they should be recorded onto a tracking mechanism for future reference. While this may be an intricate project management tool, it could just as easily be a simple spreadsheet. This tool will be used to assist with ongoing management of your project portfolio, so you will include other information as well. An example is provided in FIGURE 8.3.

## FIGURE 8.3 – PROJECT SPREADSHEET SAMPLE

**Project Proposals**

| Project | IMPACT SCORE | | | | | EFFORT SCORE | | | | |
| --- | --- | --- | --- | --- | --- | --- | --- | --- | --- | --- |
| | Hard Savings | Number of Task Owners | Scope | Strategic Connection | Impact Score | Project Expense | Time to Complete | Functions Impacted | IT System Impact | Effort Score |
| Revised Compensation Plan | Under $10k | 10 – 25 | Global | 1 | 5 | $1K to $5K | >3 months | 2 | None | 4 |
| College Recruiting | $10k to $100k | Under 10 | Regional | 2 | 0 | Less than $1K | <1 month | 1 | None | 0 |
| | | | | | 0 | | | | | 0 |
| | | | | | 0 | | | | | 0 |

Next, the scores should be plotted together on an effort/impact matrix, as seen in FIGURE 8.4. This tool provides a visual representation of the project options. By the placement of the options on the chart, it also aids in selection.

## FIGURE 8.4 – EFFORT/IMPACT MATRIX

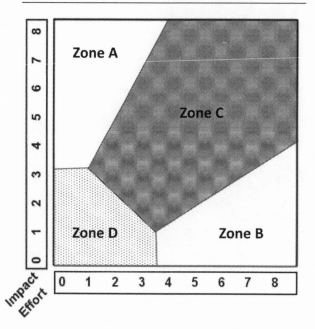

In each category of effort and impact, projects receive a score of zero, one, or two—low, medium, and high scores. The projects will score zero to eight on the impact scale (the vertical axis of FIGURE 8.4) and the effort scale (the horizontal axis). Plotting the points on the chart will place the project in one of the four zones on the chart.

Zone A are high-impact, low-effort projects, the low-hanging fruit discussed in a previous chapter. These should be fifty percent or more of your portfolio, especially in the early stages. These will provide you with quick wins, immediate value, and credibility to undertake long-term change. Those projects are likely to be found in Zone B, the high-value projects with considerable complexity. Due to the nature of these projects and the time it will likely take to execute them, your most seasoned project managers will be best deployed here. Zone B projects should start at no more than twenty-five percent of your total portfolio, though this may increase as your practice matures.

Zone C projects, low impact with high effort, are best avoided if possible. They can slow down your progress and drain your resources. You can examine these ideas to see if there are ways to break up the project into smaller, more management pieces. Then you can examine them again, so they should not be simply discarded. Zone C will also likely contain your compliance-related projects, which may force their way into your plan. You should make every effort to keep these as less than ten percent of your portfolio.

Finally, Zone D are low-effort, low-impact projects. These are sometimes known as "Just Do It" projects. They can often be executed by a team leader with little or no project experience, thanks to their simplicity, short duration, and relative lack of importance. They are an excellent talent-development opportunity and should make up ten to fifteen percent of your portfolio overall.

## KEY PROJECT ROLES

Once you have plotted your projects and decided what to pursue, the next step is to determine who will serve as the project champion and who will be the team leader.

The role of champion is one of the most critical, yet misunderstood, in the project management world. Simply put, the project champion is the member of the leadership team who is responsible for ensuring project completion and returns the expected value or greater. This often means making high-level decisions, signing off on each major project phase, removing obstacles, and acquiring the resources necessary for success. Many project champions abdicate a great deal of their responsibility to the team leader, trusting they will do the work required to be successful, and therefore limiting the champion's role to an occasional status discussion. Projects with this kind of leadership will suffer from an extremely high-failure rate.

Project leaders are responsible for organizing the team, assigning the tasks, and following up on action items. They are also generally responsible for rooting out any issues that may derail the project and bringing them to the champion, as well as keeping them informed on progress. They are usually well versed in the project management discipline followed by the organization. They are also capable of leading large group discussions, facilitating change management work, and resolving conflict in a productive way. Depending on the complexity and scope, project leadership is likely to be a full-time role in your organization.

The champion and the project leader should be in close contact during the project execution. The champion should make a habit of asking tough, probing questions of the project leader to help make sure the project is not only progressing but is doing so with the best possible results. Many champions fail at this task, as some people naturally avoid conflict and prefer to be simply supportive instead. The truth is that asking those probing questions of the champion are critical to the project's success. They should not be viewed as a simple a criticism of the champion's work. Project leaders should seek these questions if the team leader is not asking them and should be comfortable with not knowing the answers. The pursuit of this information will go far in your overall efforts toward a successful and impactful portfolio.

## STAYING ORGANIZED

One of the great challenges of running any project is figuring out who does what. A RACI (or RASCI, depending on which version you use) chart is a great tool to help you get your team priorities and activities in line.

RACI is an acronym for the different levels of engagement in any project activity.

**R – Responsible to perform the task**

**A – Accountable for the task being completed**

**C – Consulted with prior to the activity being performed**

**I – Informed that the task has been completed**

Every task will have some combination of these levels, but not always all five. (Some charts add the Support role as well. I prefer to stick with RACI for the sake of simplicity.) Let's take a look at how these roles might be applied to a project task, such as in FIGURE 8.5.

### FIGURE 8.5

| Step | Task | R | A | C | I |
|------|------|---|---|---|---|
| 1 | Create Project Charter | D, JK | JK | TS, MO | |
| 2 | Distribute Charter for comments | JK | JK | | DJ, TS |
| 3 | Schedule approval meeting | DJ, JK | JK | TS | |
| 4 | Lead approval meeting | JK, TS | TS | | |
| 5 | Schedule project kickoff session | DJ | JK | TS | TS |
| 6 | Distribute approved Charter | DJ | TS | | JK, MO |
| 7 | Publish meeting minutes | DJ | JK | | TS |
| 8 | | | | | |
| 9 | | | | | |

*Responsible* — This is the person or persons doing the work. If you have a team of experts working on a revised compensation platform, they are Responsible to make sure the policies are written, reviewed, and sensible.

Many hands make the work light, it is said, and so it is not uncommon to see many *Rs* on a task.

*Accountable* — For any task, someone is in charge of getting it done. This might be the Compensation Director, the project manager, or the IT resource leader. If you only have one person working on the task, they may have the *R* and the *A* assigned to them. But if there is a team, someone coordinates that work and makes sure it is done.

It has been said that if everyone is accountable, no one is. In project work, this is often the case. So while you have many *Rs*, there can only be one *A*. They are the Highlander of the project task.

*Consulted* — You will often have important tasks in a project that must be complete before the next step starts, as well as communications to stakeholders before work on a new task begins. In our compensation example, we may need to make sure we have buy-in from executives on which behaviors we want to incentivize in our workforce. We may need to Consult with our leaders to make sure our assumptions are correct and align with the business strategy.

Multiple *Cs* often exist for a task, depending on the level of complexity of the task. Hopefully those interested parties are part of the normal project communications.

*Informed* — When the work is done, we need to let others know. In this example, we may need to let the policy manager know we no longer need the previous version, and that we should replace all public postings with the new plan. Indicating the *Is* on our chart makes sure we know to whom that communication should be sent.

*Support* — The optional role of the chart. These are people who make sure the task owners are successful. *Support* role in our example might be the Talent Management team who helps define the right incentives, the HR leader who can help provide additional resources as needed, all the way down to the administrative assistant who makes sure the team has ample coffee and materials to stay productive.

I prefer to leave this role out of the chart, as I mentioned, for simplicity. Most of these roles are either captured in the *Rs* or *Cs*, or are not really part of the project team. If you feel the need to include them though, I won't judge you.

## PROJECT TIMING AND LEADERSHIP

I once worked with an organization that looked upon project leadership as a tremendous opportunity to develop talent. They built rigorous structure around Six Sigma training, and entrance into the program was generally reserved for those identified as "high potential." Those top performers would be sent through a four-month program to gain knowledge and experience in improvement techniques. They would then be tasked with finding improvement opportunities in their part of the business, which would, in theory, cover the cost of the training program. Then they returned to their regular roles with the additional task to run the improvement projects to completion. In many cases, though, these were the same people who were looked upon as the best candidates to move up into new roles as they were opened, usually in a stretch assignment designed to push their abilities.

Suddenly, their chosen projects, which were normally closely related to their original job, were no longer important to them, and they dedicated their time to their new roles. The project champion, generally a member of the business unit leadership team, would be understanding and allow them to drop the project, at least in the short term. Those projects, of course, were never picked back up. The truth was the projects only really mattered in the context of completing the training, and with the project leader being promoted, no one was terribly interested in pursuing the opportunity further. This company, as you might expect, suffered from terribly low project completion rates and low returns compared to projections.

The solutions to this problem were to stop allowing project leaders to find their own projects and to put a limit on the number of people sent to training. Instead, projects were generated in deployment sessions as outlined above and were owned by the project champion. They selected team leaders based on skillsets and project needs, and new project leaders were trained only as a skill gap was identified. Finally, the champion was expected to be confident enough in the project's value that they would be willing to reduce their operating budget by at least fifty percent of the expected first year project savings. Any project that didn't inspire that level of confidence was left for further discussion. The champion would then move forward with a project they felt would be worth pursuing and would find the right team leader for the job. This kind of project ownership will be critical for the success of your own portfolio and should be incorporated from the start.

It is also important to review projects based on likely timelines for start and end dates. For some topics, such as open enrollment or college recruiting, you need to take into consideration certain dates for making a change. With those identified up front, as seen in FIGURE 8.6, the remaining projects can be scheduled during available periods. Proposed team leaders can also be aligned with this schedule, helping ensure no individual will be overtaxed in the planning stage and their available time will be used wisely.

FIGURE 8.6 – PROJECT TIMING AND DECISIONS

## Project Proposals

| Project | Timing | | Time Commitment (Leader) | Decision (Go/No Go/Hold) | Charter Due Date (Champion) |
| | Start Date | End Date | | | |
|---|---|---|---|---|---|
| Revised Compensation Plan | N/A | N/A | 100% | Go | January 31 |
| College Recruiting | January 1 | August 1 | 25% | Go | November 1 |
| | | | | | |

Finally, give consideration to any special skills that might be necessary for the team, such as an expert in regulatory areas, system programming, supply chain, or another discipline. With discussion points recorded for future reference, you should reach a decision as a team about which projects to pursue, which to hold, and which to reject. Finally, set a date for the completion of the project charter—a task that is owned by the project champion. This document, which exists in multiple formats, is intended to clearly several key components of the project:

- **Objective:** This is the short explanation, or elevator speech, that outlines what the project aims to accomplish. For example, *"The objective of this project is to implement the software tools necessary for dramatic improvements in the throughput, cycle time, and cost of providing HR support to employees. The project will be considered complete when the software has been selected, tested, and implemented across the organization, which should be complete in less than three months. Success will determined by a high rate of adoption and a measurable reduction in request resolution times for employees."*

- **Context:** This is the second element of the elevator speech, intended to explain the reason a change is needed. *"With the increasing ratio of employees to HR FTEs, there is a need to improve overall efficiency to maintain an appropriately high level of service. With no central system of record keeping for case management work, comparison to previous conversations, and collaboration within the team become difficult—if not impossible—to support. While the processes themselves have been reviewed and improved, an opportunity exists to leverage new technology to achieve greater results."*

- **Goals:** These outline the initial metrics that will be used to define success, and the targets that are built into the project assumptions. *"Implementing this type of tool is expected to result in an increase in first-call resolution of at least twenty-five percent, and reduce overall call length by fifty percent. Long term, this will allow the team to support an increase of up to twenty-five percent in the employee population without the need to add additional HR headcount."*

- **Deliverables:** These are the concrete outcomes that are expected from the completed project. *"Upon completion, a new software package will have been deployed across the HR organization, including a regularly scheduled HR training class, documentation including both a user's guide and on-screen help, and a knowledge base populated with all current HR polices and procedures. This system will also include a full data interface with both out primary employee record, our payroll software, and our training software."*

- **Scope:** This shows what is part of the project and what is not. A clearly expressed scope will greatly increase the chance of success by avoiding additional tasks being added to the project. *"The project is limited to the software to be used by the HR team in relation to employee requests and needs and will not be concerned with the related HR systems to* *which it will interface. It will also not include changes to HR policies, with the exception of any directly related to use of this system."*

The far-left column of FIGURE 8.5 indicates the charter due date, which is the final stage in the portfolio selection process. When this is complete, you should have a calendar that includes the projects to be pursued, the champion of each project, a proposed project leader, and an identified charter completion date for each item on the list. You are now ready to begin the work of project execution!

## SUMMARY

Selecting the right projects is as important as all of the work done in identifying and investigating opportunities. Reviewing options as a team, comparing projects, and choosing those with the best impact to effort ratio will give you the best chance of long-term success. With engaged champions, who own the project and provide the required resources; the right team leaders for the project tasks; and an awareness of critical timing throughout the year, you can build a solid plan. By selecting the right portfolio mix of short-term and long-term projects, you can expect value to be delivered throughout your portfolio lifecycle. Finally, each deployment session needs to end with a list of projects that everyone agreed upon and the task of creating the project charter with a clear completion date.

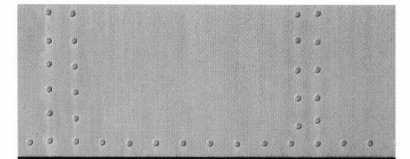

# 9
# PROJECT PORTFOLIO GENERATION – CONTROL

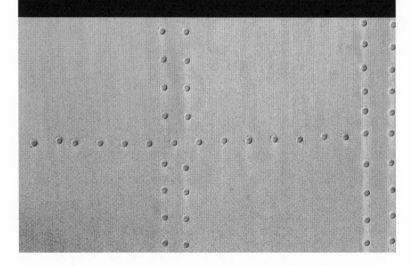

● ● ●

The "final" phase of generating your portfolio is control. This is the ongoing work that ensures projects are progressing, the necessary resources are being deployed, and new ideas are continuously being generated.

## TRACKING MECHANISM

By now you probably understand the primary metrics your organization tracks regarding project value. Equally important is the way in which project savings are measure and reported, as well as the way progress will be monitored and shared.

One of the most common forms of project tracking is known as a "stage gate" review. This requires the division of each project into major milestones, each of which must be affirmed as successfully completed by the project champion before additional work can be done. The DMAIC model is one example of this division, though it is also very common to have major tasks defined as the key milestone. A sample project plan with task-based, stage-gate milestones is shown in FIGURE 9.1.

## FIGURE 9.1 – PROJECT MILESTONES AND APPROVALS

| Task Number | Task | Owner | Due | Delivered? |
|---|---|---|---|---|
| 1 | Project Approval | DT | 1/1 | Y |
| 1.1 | Budget set, accounts in place | DT | 1/31 | Y |
| 1.2 | Gate 1 approved as complete | DT | 1/31 | Y |
| 2 | Project Team Identified | ABS | 2/14 | Y |
| 2.1 | Team approved and notified | ABS | 2/28 | Y |
| 2.2 | Workloads reassigned, travel approved | ABS | 3/15 | Y |
| 2.3 | Gate 2 approved as complete | DT | 3/22 | Y |
| 3 | Project Kickoff | ABS | 4/1 | |
| 3.1 | Charter reviewed and approved | ABS | 4/3 | |
| 3.2 | Initial work assignments accepted | ABS | 4/5 | |
| 3.3 | Gate 3 approved as complete | ABS | 4/7 | |

The project champion and leader will need to decide together how often a formal project review is required. If there is a close working relationship between the two, formal reviews will be less frequent. Otherwise, sessions should be scheduled no less than monthly and may be held as frequently as each week. Whatever the schedule, be sure you allow enough time for the project to progress between sessions to make sure there is value in reviewing the status. Whatever frequency you set, there are a few things that should be on the agenda for each meeting.

- **Current progress to plan:** How far along in the project did you expect to be, and how far along are you? While it is neither unique nor catastrophic for a project plan to go off track at some point, you should have the expectation of staying close to the schedule if you are to meet delivery dates. Keeping a close eye on any variance from the beginning will help the champion determine when additional resources are needed.

- **Upcoming key tasks:** What needs to happen next in the project plan? Are all the prerequisites completed? Forward-looking discussions help avoid focusing on any failures or delays, and keep the project framed in a positive light. It also sets up the summary discussion around support needed by the project leader at the end of the session.

- **Performance of team:** The project leader should be prepared to give a brief summary of team performance, including any conflict with their normal job duties. It is not unusual for a team member's "day job" to interfere with project work, especially as key milestones approach. To help support them, monitor their performance, and adjust their involvement level as needed.

- **Identified risks:** There will come a time in every project when success is threatened by one or more outside influences. This could be a competing project, a change in the business plan, losing a team member, or other unforeseen event. It is critical that these be identified and assessed on a regular basis to allow for mitigating action to be planned.

- **Next steps:** This should encompass mitigation plans for any delays that have happened as well as any identified risks. Planned actions should be built with the expectation that the project will be on track, or at least partially caught up, by the next review session. This should include not just the activity of the project leader, but also the tasks assigned to the team members and the project champion as well.

- **Support needed:** No project champion should ever leave a review without asking, "How can I help?" And no project leader should fail to have a list at the ready. Involved champions always knows how they add to the project and are ready to acquire resources or support in the organization when given the chance. It is critical they know at the end of each session how they can best help and are ready to update the project leader on their success as well.

## CONTROLLING THE SCOPE

You will, in the course of overseeing projects, be pushed at times on the limits of your boundaries. We document them up front to avoid scope creep, but that doesn't mean there aren't times where adding an additional goal or measure is wrong. To help, here are a few way to analyze potential creep and determine if it belongs in your project.

- Is the task/feature/assignment critical to the overall project deliverable? Critical in this case means the project will be deemed a failure without it.

- Was the task/feature/assignment included in the vision of the project? This is not necessarily the project definition document, by the way. Those miss things all the time. When you were under the table and dreaming, did visions of this change dance in your head?

- Are the people best qualified to solve the problem or deliver said goods part of the project team?

- Can the task/feature/assignment be discussed in project meetings without a team member gagging, wheezing or resigning?

If you answered "no" to any of these, it might be scope creep. If you answered "no" to all of them, it is certainly creepy. Throw some cold water at the person pushing the idea and get yourself (and your project) back on track.

## PROJECT CLOSURE

Along with the management of ongoing projects, certain responsibilities belong to the project champion involving project completion. By definition, a project is not an ongoing set of tasks and will at some point need to be "finished." To reach that goal, the champion will need to oversee several steps.

First, the team needs the chance to present its progress and celebrate both success and failure. Celebration of success is a bit obvious. However, acknowledging the failures of a project as a chance to learn, rather than a reason to admonish, will have an incredible impact on your culture. The motto of many Lean practitioners is to "try stuff, break stuff, and make stuff better." In an environment that recognizes the value of risk, even in a failed attempt, the thrill of discovery will outweigh the fear of failure.

Second, the team must understand that they are expected to present additional ideas for the next improvement cycle. It is remarkably rare that a project team does not bump up against their scope a few times during project execution. Teams need to be aware of those events and plan to present them during the final report as the next set of opportunities to review. Building this pipeline of ideas will also ensure that your portfolio is never lacking for bottom-up improvement opportunities. You will also know before starting which members of the team found those ideas and can consider them as team leaders for their projects, if selected.

Finally, the leadership team needs to acknowledge the success or failure of the project, recognize the effort put in by the project team, and officially release them from their responsibilities. Good team members are the lifeblood of a project portfolio, but they need to be returned to the wild, so to speak, from time to time. This will allow them to refocus on their primary duties with a new perspective, perhaps finding immediate opportunities to eliminate waste in their normal role. The ability to identify and get rid of excess waste every day is a major benefit of project work. Your goal should be to have as many members of your organization learn this ability as possible.

Some organizations put a great deal of time, effort, and money into a small token of appreciation for a project. This could be a certificate, backpack, or pen set. One of the most interesting suggestions I've heard was to present each team member with a thank you letter. To make it special, the leadership team decided to include pictures of themselves as well. Seriously. We convinced them that a thank you gift was only valuable if the recipient thought it was. They decided to give each person a laptop bag with the company logo and project named embroidered on the front. The letter went inside.

Without diving too deeply into the theory behind motivation, it's probably fair to say these gifts are appreciated as recognition. Sometimes, however, a simple "thank you" will often suffice. The best way for the organization to show employees they are valued is to invest some or all of the project savings back into the company, either through pay increases, bonus pay, or even funding for projects that focus on the employee experience, such as an upgrade to the break room or green space. These projects do not return dollars to the bottom line in most cases and so are purely for the benefit of the employees. Investing in them is one of the strongest ways to show your appreciation as a leadership team.

## SUMMARY

Tracking the progress of a project should be an active role for champions, and their regular status meetings with the team leader should cover several important components, including upcoming milestones and potential risks. The champion's role is not just to listen, but also to be active in clearing obstacles for the team.

# 10
# STARTING YOUR JOURNEY

●  ●  ●

With the ability to build a project portfolio and examine ideas in hand, it is worth taking a look at the traditional structure of HR and how Lean can further drive performance. Lean is more than simple tools and a commonsense approach to eliminating waste. Lean is also a mindset that everyone involved in a process—workers, designers, suppliers, and customers—should be involved in making it better. With that in mind, here are a few approaches inspired by the Lean world that may aid in building your own roadmap to the future.

## COOPERATIVE PROCESS DESIGN

Toyota pioneered the concept of designing systems in partnership with their vendors. A traditional design process once consisted of engineers working together to recreate a steering, braking, or transmission system. Once the design was finished, they would publish specifications for each part, and then suppliers would be given the opportunity to bid for the contract to supply parts. In most cases, the work was awarded to the low bidder. Toyota found there to be a great deal of waste and conflict in this approach and took a different path.

In many cases, Toyota components are designed with their customers, who define the value. Suppliers, who are experts in the craft and use of individual components, also help design them. Rather than base their purchasing decisions on who could best meet the part specifications developed without input, Toyota believed that suppliers could make the design more efficient. Therefore they could reduce the overall cost to build that system. By involving their internal customers, such as related automotive systems or functions, they could produce a better overall product for the market.

HR has a similar opportunity to build stronger systems internally. Too often, HR is divided into functional teams that concentrate on their own work, not the holistic work of the department. This is even more pronounced when dealing with external resources, such as a third-party recruiter. They are assigned a discrete task that may have significant ramifications to talent management or long-term business plans, yet they are not aware of those aspects of the job.

To really drive value, we should view our processes in terms of the upstream and downstream impacts and involved interested parties in the planning and execution stages. External recruiters can make better recommendations if they understand your needs not just for today, but also for the next five years. Bringing talent that can help build the business faster and stronger benefits everyone, but they need exposure to the business plan and in some cases, succession planning, to do so.

### SHARED IMPROVEMENT EXPECTATIONS

The target of any improvement plan is to get everyone involved without tracking, much the same way as law enforcement is only effective when the public is voluntarily compliant. Building a culture that celebrates both success and failure is one component to getting there. Another important piece is an expectation that everyone participates in change.

We have all worked with naysayers who are happy to point out why a change won't work. They are usually just as happy to explain all the great things they could be doing if only there weren't so many other things to do. As a project leader or champion, that's exactly what you want to hear!

The most effective way to harness this negative energy is to have an open discussion about what everyone would like to be doing. Rarely will the answers involve doing paperwork, answering repetitive emails, or listening to complaints. Instead you will hear about strategic work, meaningful improvements, and challenging tasks that never seem to be the top priority. Track these lovingly, for they will be your future.

Next, discuss what is holding each person back. What are the jobs that take up the most time? What is non-value added, in Lean terms, that could be eliminated? What tasks could you eliminate that would never impact your clients? That list is just as important.

With those two task lists in hand, challenge the team to work towards eliminating one so the other can be achieved. This will be accomplished through project work, in some cases, and in individual effort in others. But either way, take time in team meetings to ask, "What have you done to make this different?" The most vocal opponents of change are usually not clear how they will benefit from it, and they are able to avoid responsibility for making change on their own. Letting them define the path, then holding them accountable will give them power and aid your progress.

## ATTACK SACRED COWS

As covered in previous chapters, the ability to ask questions that may seem obvious, or just asking "why?" several times, can lead to unexpected answers. Just as interesting, though, is challenging the previously unquestioned in your organization.

Every company has a product, process, or person that is considered beyond reproach. It is accepted at face value, and dealt with as an immutable fact. But what if it weren't? What could you possibly damage by asking questions? What you will often find is that the answers are long forgotten, or at least a lot less relevant than they once were.

This is not, of course, a suggestion that you should upset the status quo for the sake of creating conflict. That can be a career-limiting move, to be sure. Instead, practice the art of positive inquiry, or questioning specifically how to improve a situation. This approach, coupled with respect for history and the progress you have already made, will allow you to gain insight into some of the basic assumptions of your business and culture.

## STRETCH GOALS

For those who have been through any kind of strategic planning, personal development planning, project planning or party planning, you have certainly had to set a goal. And usually with goals come a nebulous idea of "stretch" goals. Stretch goals are intentionally hard to reach, maybe even impossible. But some people aren't comfortable with putting down a goal that can't be reached. That's understandable. Why set yourself up for failure? Maybe there should be goals, big goals and then stretch goals. But I think a better solution is to perhaps define what a stretch goals really is, and what it should represent.

In *Blue Ocean Strategy*, one of my favorite business books, there is a great review of the business transformation of Swatch watches. They took a whole new approach to their industry, starting with the idea of their price point first, then working backward through their process to get to profit. It's a great story, and a great example of stretch. If you put a 75% reduction of production costs in the strategic plan, you'd have some nervous people in the room. And they did. Then they made it happen.

At the start, Nicholas Hayek, chairman of Swatch, set up a project team to determine the strategic price for the Swatch... Swatch set the price at $40, a price at which most people could buy multiple Swatches as fashion accessories. The low price left no profit margin for Japanese or Hong Kong-based companies to copy Swatch and undercut its price.

Instead of using more traditional metal or leather, for example, Swatch used plastic. Swatch's engineers also drastically simplified the design of the watch's inner workings, reducing the number of parts from one hundred fifty to fifty-one. Finally, the engineers developed new and cheaper assembly techniques...Taken together, the design and manufacturing changes enabled Swatch to reduce direct labor costs from thirty percent to less than ten percent of total cots.

When I think stretch goals, I think of stories like that. Incredible tales of what Jim Collins would call a BHAG (big, hairy, audacious goal) and the teams who reach them. His epic *Good to Great* is full of them. There are a lot of stories between those two books, many of them about teams that did what looked impossible.

Why do I bring it up? Because when I think of stretch goals, I think of these stories. And the lesson is this:

> **If you reach your stretch goals, someone will write a book about them. And you.**

Think your goals aren't worthy of being preserved as lessons to future leaders? Then maybe they aren't really stretch. Maybe they are just big goals. There's nothing inherently wrong with that. We should all have big goals. But you might want to scribble down a stretch goal or two as well. You don't even have to tell anyone about it. Just know they exist. Because if they don't, you'll never reach them.

All the tools in the world won't help you make a radical change alone. The reason we've discussed the need to include small, quick-win projects in your portfolio is that they are required to help you establish credibility and momentum. These projects are critical because, regardless of how clear it is you can improve your practice, they will meet resistance. Take heart in knowing that you can overcome it, leading to a real change in your culture. As Teddy Roosevelt once said about politics, "It takes a long time to overcome inertia, and that, when it has been overcome, it takes an equally long time to stop momentum."

With that in mind, let's look briefly at the challenge you'll face in starting your continuous improvement journey.

## SOCIAL INERTIA

An interesting phenomenon is taking place in the business world, or pretty much in any other gathering of individuals. You've likely experienced it repeatedly in long business meetings with no clear agenda. Everyone in the room is dissatisfied with the situation, yet no one vocalizes the issue.

It is terribly common and frighteningly powerful. I like to think of it as social inertia. The amount of shared pain we experience somehow suppresses our urge to speak up.

I was invited to a two-day workshop with my extended teammates for a large organization. I would guess there were fifty people in attendance, from the vice president down to the frontline call center members. Our general topic was innovation, and we had invited in a guest speaker who had a great deal of experience in the area. The next eight hours were, by way of general consensus, sheer torture.

It wasn't great that the guest speaker was difficult to follow. It wasn't terrific that he insisted on showing us videos that were ten to twenty years old. It wasn't desirable to spend an hour listening to him tell us how good he was at his job. It was mildly amusing when he shushed the VP, who was commenting that she couldn't hear him. But more than anything, it wasn't productive. We spent the first half of the day brainstorming ideas to work on. When we all agreed on what we wanted to fix, we ended up with twenty or so "big ideas" for change. But we never discussed any of them after that day, let alone considered them for implementation.

Two highlights from that workshop, however, have stayed with me to this day. First was our lunch break. It was a beautiful day, as I recall, and everyone headed outside to enjoy the sunshine. I was one of the last out and walked through the door just in time to catch the end of the exchange between the VP and my director. Here's what I heard.

"I hate him. Are we going to spend all day like this?" said the VP.

My director received this with stumbling and stammering and a promise it would get better. That director, by the way, was the one who had booked the speaker. As you may have guessed, it did not actually get any better, which makes the second highlight that much more interesting.

At day's end, we were all given a T-shirt emblazoned with the speaker's name and logo, and were asked to step outside for a group photo. We had seen several of these photos at the beginning of the day, and I remembered how everyone in these large groups looked like they were having a good time. It was only then I realized their faces were frozen in a ghoulish grimace, and they were mostly relieved the day was over. (That was my guess, anyway.)

Everyone shirted up and gathered outside to become marketing material. Not everyone was excited about it, even though apparently our enthusiasm was contractually obligated. They pushed us together and admonished us for not smiling enough. We were also instructed (not asked) to throw up epic jazz hands to create the impression of enthusiasm.

And who was pushing us into this crime of misrepresentation that would be perpetrated on future teams? It was none other than the VP herself. The pressure to "go along to get along" applies to leaders as well.

It can reach beyond the moment as well. Later I learned that we did not actually pay that speaker for his time. Instead, we had agreed to send two people to an extended version of the same workshop later that year. The chosen two were horrified at spending more time with this person. Still, they had no intention of backing out, despite the fact that no one enjoyed the class, no value had been gained, and no one thought it would be worth having these two essentially out of action for a week.

You will run into this when you attempt to change any of the traditional models of HR activity. I was once part of an HR department that spent weeks preparing to discuss the idea of maybe changing the date of our merit increase cycle. We did not discuss the change but prepared to discuss it. It took that long because even though we had good reasons for the HR team, the operations team, and the employees, we couldn't move past the idea that we had "always done it that way." We could expect the same responses if we had started discussions to change the way we approached open enrollment, talent reviews, or development plans. Having an established system is sometimes the toughest thing you will have to overcome.

Inertia is powerful indeed.

## RED FLAGS

To deal with resistance, you must first identify the causes. This will usually mean people and usually those on your team. Fortunately, there are patterns of behavior for which you can watch to detect potential issues early. Having an idea of what obstacles you may find and how to get around them will greatly increase your changes of success. But always remember that people are creative, and there will always be new sources of challenges waiting for you, no matter how many projects you have run.

I've worked with high-level leaders on project teams that did not understand the standard process idea. They liked the work of mapping a process and were even intrigued by the tools we used to make some decisions. But when it came time to implement and see a real difference in the way we operate, they became skittish. They were not truly vested in the change and therefore not willing to put their own political capital and credibility on the line. Trying to make a change with leaders who aren't fully on board is a sure path toward failure.

I've also had functional leaders on the team that did not understand our goal was to create a standard process across the business. In one case, they actually said, "Go ahead and design it. I'll make changes for my team when you are done."

What do you do in that case? We stopped the session and invited that person to leave. After all, if you can't commit yourself to working toward a shared solution, how can you create one? They stayed, apologized for their misstep, and promised to work together. Predictably, they went back and modified the standard process two months later in their own division.

Worst of all, though, are those in the room and on the team who do nothing to voice their opinions or displeasure. Occasionally, the disgruntled team member will let personal feelings be known through body language and non-verbal cues. Any facilitator or team leader will be able to pick up on those things and invite them to share their feelings. But those who remain silent, withholding key pieces of information? They are the ones who will sink your ship every time. As the saying goes, "It's the quiet ones you have to watch." In the case of process design, it is absolutely true.

How do you deal with these red flags? Each situation is different, but here are a few tips to help keep your projects on track.

*Be direct.* Humans are programmed, in large part, to be polite and avoid conflict. Fight the urge to say nothing or, worse, address the entire group instead of the individual. If you have a problem child on the team, let that person know directly that their behavior is disruptive. If there is no change, remove that person from the team. The other members will appreciate it.

If you are dealing with champions or other leaders, it's a bit trickier. You may not have the option of excusing them from the project or team. But being direct is still usually the best approach. Outline your needs and align your expectations. If they won't or can't give you the support you need, they aren't truly invested in the project. Sometimes, you have to recognize that and move on to the next opportunity.

*Use their momentum.* One of the core concepts of Aikido is to move in harmony with your attacker, using as much of their energy and as little of yours as possible. The same could be said for dealing with resistors on your team. Especially useful are those that voice their opinions and try to push their beliefs. These individuals are the ones who truly want standards, as long as the standards are theirs. By guiding them down the path of discovery, you can let them "find" the best ways to improve, and then let them drive the change. Their energy will become one of your greatest assets, and they will become your fans.

**Give in.** Resistors can be a lot of things. They can be exasperating, they can be scheming, and they can be your worst nightmare.

But they can also be right.

One of the dirty secrets about process design is that you won't think of everything, and you won't think of everyone. There will be people involved in your process that have been forgotten or haven't been involved, and they will not feel beholden to your design. They will do what they feel is right to get their job done, which is not always what you have planned. When that happens, it is a sure sign that you missed something.

Some people will color outside the lines out of spite. But for the most part, people want to do their job well but with no more effort than is necessary.

(This is not to say they are lazy, just that they are human. People who want to put in extra effort for the same outcome should be watched very carefully, in my opinion, and should probably be kept away from sharp objects.) Especially in the early stages of implementing change, you may find those who don't follow the process and do things "their way." Watch them, listen to them, and try to learn. They may have a better idea after all.

## SUMMARY

Your journey will not be easy, but there are incredible opportunities waiting to be found. Looking at the breakthrough ideas from Lean organizations is one way to find inspiration. You will still likely find you are constrained by resources, not by the lack of opportunity. The quick-win projects will not only building momentum, they will free up resources that you can use to perpetuate your improvement work.

There will be obstacles, of course, and those around you will generate most of them. React wisely, and you might turn those problem children into your greatest assets!

# 11
# PREPARE
# FOR LAUNCH

This book started with a discussion about changes in business and how your environment has shifted over the last decade. The "good old days," in truth, weren't all that good most of the time. And they aren't coming back.

We are now in a new business environment that appreciates value, problem solving, and the ability to make changes for the better. The days of lifetime employment, which allowed workers to put their head down for twenty years, are gone. Instead, we are in a dynamic environment that will reward those who move quickly and constantly evolve.

The skills discussed in this book will help you do those things. Understanding waste, knowing how to recognize it, and having an idea of how to eliminate it are the price of admission for a serious career. Being able to leverage those skills into a portfolio of projects, leading others to make changes and drastically magnify your own impact, is invaluable. Knowing how to lead the organization into a change mindset will make you a very important influence in your organization's future.

## INTERNAL NETWORKING

There are few things more powerful than a strong network. This is especially true in the workplace, as the audience is limited by the size of your company. The opportunity to magnify your message with key supporters can be more powerful than the original idea. It would behoove you to start immediately on cultivating a network of trust, building up your political capital and credibility before you need them.

Building this network doesn't have to be done with a haphazard approach. We often look at our lives as a series of events that have, through happenstance, led us to maintain a circle of friends. In the workplace, you can't rely on chance to put you in touch with the right people at the right time. Networking, internal or external, is an activity that requires determination and focus to execute properly.

First, it is important to identify the influencers in your organization. Depending on the size and number of employees, the level of difficulty will vary. Fortunately, the first step is usually the same. Simply make a list of the people from whom you receive trusted information, or to whom you reach out when you need to know something. Building upon that existing relationship, start asked your influencers where their information comes from. Lather, rinse, repeat.

You'll soon have a decent map of how information flows through your organization. It won't be perfect, and it won't static, but you should be able to sketch out a basic hub-and-spoke diagram, such as in FIGURE 11.1. Each circle represents an influencer, and the size of the circle gives you a visual representation of how many people trust them to provide information. These, then, are the people to whom you should speak about potential projects and changes. If they speak well of your ideas, they have a much better chance of finding success. If they oppose you, you may be better off looking for a new project.

**FIGURE 11.1**

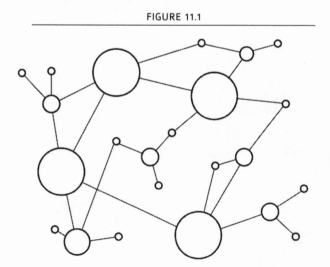

Once you have your network mapped, it is time to work on cultivating your level of trust with those prime influencers. The best way to do so is to provide something of value to them. Humans are wired for reciprocity, and giving of yourself is the quickest way to enhance your relationship with others. This needn't be done in a disingenuous way, but should instead be done with sincerity and enthusiasm for the task. Find projects or tasks that you believe in, help make them successful, and you will end up with a stronger relationship and organization.

Building that network of trust will accomplish two goals. They will hopefully help you with building momentum, but they will also be critical in giving you candid and robust feedback on your ideas. The worst kind of network for a Lean practitioner is the one that wants to succeed so badly, they tell you every idea is a winner and send you out the door. You need those who will tell you when your baby is ugly, so to speak, and help you avoid mistakes by delivering honest advice at every step.

## CONFRONTING THE ENEMY

As an agent of change, you will encounter resistance on a regular basis. You should learn to be comfortable with it early, as it will be a big part of your daily adventure. One thing you can do to help is to understand why people are resistant to change, and then how to help them embrace it.

In his book *Bare Bones Change Management: What you shouldn't not do*, Bob Lewis takes a look at the idea that people are "naturally" change resistant, and offers a wonderful explanation of what's really happening:

> **For the most part, people don't resist change. What they resist is change they expect to be unpleasant, which is an entirely different matter. A lot of what's characterized as "natural resistance to change" is actually natural resistance to he imposition of disagreeable circumstances, such as layoffs, longer work hours, the invalidation of hard-won skills, the redesign of responsibilities in ways that make work boring and dreary...in other words, the outcome of just about every business change employees have had to**

**deal with over the past few decades. And here you come along with another one. In the absence of convincing information, what conclusion would you expect smart employees to reach?**

Employees are resistant because they have had negative outcomes in the past, and have become not just gun-shy but skeptical of any claims you might make. You can tell them how great the outcome of your project will be, but you aren't likely to sing them a tune they've not heard before.

Your network may help overcome some of these difficulties, but you will eventually be face-to-face with a room full of doubters, the future victims of change. How do you get them interested in your vision?

One simple approach I've used is to live by our creed that value is defined by the customer. As key stakeholders, they are customers of the process and of your project design, and therefore are critical to the decisions you will make about your goals and directions. When starting with any new group, I will often gather their thoughts on what the future state should look like, independent of any project discussion.

As an example, I worked with an HR team that was preparing to implement employee self-service. I had been warned previously that the group and the culture were both very change resistant, and getting them to willingly be part of the transition would be a major obstacle. Even though our goal was to reduce the administrative work in their lives, they weren't

We started our session with a simple exercise. I put up a chart on the page and asked, "What do you deal with every day that takes far too much of your time?" The list was quite extensive, including things like:

- **Address changes**
- **Direct deposit forms**
- **Giving out the benefits hotline number**
- **Changing someone's phone number**

- Resetting passwords

- Looking up employee numbers

- Looking up available vacation hours

- Checking the status of a raise/bonus/promotion

- Sending emails to follow up on all of these things

Given that these were all functions that would be included in our self-service design, I was pleased to see that they required no prompting. They already knew they needed the tool we wanted to give them. Next we asked, "If not for those things, what would you spend your time doing?" Some of there answers were:

- Training

- Talent management

- Succession planning

- Performance improvement plans
  (that actually mean something)

- Getting to know the employees better

- Getting to know the business better

- Finding ways to improve myself and my team

Once I had these lists, I hung them on the wall in the front of the room. Then I started to describe the system we would build, and how the transactional work that had been filling their lives would now go through a portal, and employees would have direct access to check and change their own information. HR would be neither gate-keeper nor key master in the new world. As you may imagine, this was meant with much wailing and gnashing of teeth, especially by the longer-tenured members of the team.

"This won't work!" they cried. "There are legal reasons we have to do this ourselves!" I am always happy to review employment law in these cases, as I am far from an expert in the area. It is worth noting, though, that I have rarely found legal restrictions that mandate waste or redundancy in our processes.

"Employee's can't be trusted to do this! They'll make a lot of mistakes!" Overlooking the number of mistakes made on a daily basis in HR departments everywhere, I asked them a simple question. Do you think employees care about getting their paychecks more or less than the HR department? Of course they care more! So our task is to create a simple interface that helps them avoid making errors, not deprive them of the ability.

"These jobs are the most important thing HR does!" I enjoyed this one, mostly because they had just spent an hour telling me how much they hated the administrative overhead of their jobs.

"But if you take this away...what will be left for us to do?" This, finally, was the really important question. As Lewis said, people don't fear change. They fear change that is bad for them. And when you see a large chunk of your job duties going away, the though of your job following suit is not far behind. The truth is there are and always will be companies that are happy to employee people that fill out and process forms all day. We were no longer planning to be one of those companies.

The team had already told us what they would be working on. We had the list on the wall for them all to see. Once we moved past the surface issues and addressed what their jobs would be, we were able to build a future state vision that they not only accepted, but were excited to help build. That team not only defined the new system, they became our most vocal supporters. Our success was possible only because we took the time to get them on our side. The project became something we did with them, not to them.

Your critics and blockers are more than an obstacle. They are potentially your biggest fans. Focusing on winning them over will deliver far more in benefits than an equivalent effort spent on the masses. They are a smaller group in most cases, so the resources needed to work with them should be fewer. They are also far more likely to evangelize on behalf of your project once they are convinced it's the right thing for the company.

Will it always work? Of course not. But in most cases, it is the best place to start.

## GETTING THERE FROM HERE

Progress belongs to those who embrace and lead change. For the rest, unfortunately, there is no path back. For you, the path only leads forward. But you can't finish any journey you don't begin, so the time to start improving is right now.

Go!

Photo by Heather Bussing

# ABOUT THE AUTHOR

**Dwane Lay** spent over a decade as an HR practitioner, following an early career in operations, IT and quality. The background has given him a unique perspective on the processes that make up human resources, and the potential for improvements in efficiency and effectiveness. He is recognized as a leading authority on the application of Lean tools and techniques in Human Resources, as well as having a wealth of experience in applying business technology to improve HR processes.

Dwane holds an MBA from Lindenwood University, as well as having earned a Six Sigma Black Belt and is a certified Senior Professional of Human Resources with HCRI.

A well known presence on the HR social media landscape, he can be found on a variety of platforms, including Twitter (@DwaneLay), Facebook (facebook.com/dtlay) and LinkedIn (linkedin.com/in/dwanelay). He also writes on human resources, process design and, occasionally, comic books and moves at www.LeanHRBlog.com

Made in the USA
Charleston, SC
17 February 2015